W9-AOB-727

LOVE
ADDICTION

A Guide to Emotional Independence

Martha R. Bireda, Ph.D.

New Harbinger Publications, Inc.

Publisher's Note

This publication is designed to provide accurate and authoritative information in regard to the subject matter covered. It is sold with the understanding that the publisher is not engaged in rendering psychological, financial, legal, or other professional services. If expert assistance or counseling is needed, the services of a competent professional should be sought.

Copyright © 1990 by Martha R. Bireda
New Harbinger Publications, Inc.
5674 Shattuck Avenue
Oakland, CA 94609

All rights reserved

Cover design by SHELBY DESIGNS AND ILLUSTRATES

Printed in the United States of America

1st Printing November, 1990   7,500 copies

Dedication

To Kahli Andrews ... you are finally free.

Acknowledgments

This book has been made possible by the support, assistance, and encouragement of many others. I would therefore like to thank Barbara Quick, my editor, who skillfully helped to turn workshop notes and exercises into a book. I thank Nancy Levengood for her professional review and comments on the manuscript. I also thank my colleagues and friends, Norma Caltagirone and Bunny Napoli, for their unwavering support, beginning to end.

I wish to thank Dr. R. J. Doody and Carolyn Foster of the Juvenile Welfare Board in St. Petersburg, Florida, who, through my "Transforming Relationships" workshops, gave me the opportunity to use and develop the ideas presented in this book. Finally, I thank my children, Jaha and Saba, who made many sacrifices, and encouraged and loved me throughout this process.

Contents

About This Book

Love Addiction is a book about choosing to change your thinking and behavior, unlearning old belief systems, and replacing unhealthy behavioral patterns. Almost everyone can learn healthier ways to interact in his or her close relationships. This book will help you bring love into balance: by learning to love yourself, you will be more fully able to love another.

If you are currently involved in a painful or dead-end relationship, you may want to consider making a change. If you find that you move from one unhealthy relationship to another, you may wish to consider doing things differently in the future. If you're tired of playing the same old tapes and repeating the same patterns of failure, then this book may be of use to you.

One caveat. *Love Addiction* is primarily designed to reinforce a recovery process that has already begun. This book will be most helpful to those who are in the latter stages of recovery. I'm assuming that you already have a basic grasp of your problem, and have thought at length about the emotional issues involved in your addiction.

Recovery is a *process*. There are no quick fixes for behavioral patterns that have been developed and reinforced over many years. However, with a commitment to change, and a determination to do the work required for change to occur, you can learn to think and act in healthy ways when involved in a close relationship. You can learn to love yourself and to prepare to develop the healthy, loving, and lasting relationship you desire.

1

Love Out of Balance

Jennifer's eyes lit up when she saw David walk into the restaurant. He was here and only ten minutes late this time. As he got closer, however, she knew something was wrong. He had that "I'm sorry Jenny" look on his face—the one he got when he was about to disappoint her. David sat down, gave her a kiss, and then it came. "Jenny, honey, I feel awful about this, but I can't go away this weekend. Phil—you've heard me talk about Phil, my best friend from college—is coming into town on Saturday. He's going to be here for a week attending a convention. I've just got to see the guy," David said, trying to let Jennifer down easy.

"But, David, you promised. Every time we plan something *I* want to do, it never works out. Every single time!" David looked down and waited for Jenny to calm down and agree to another weekend—she always did. Finally, she looked up at David with tears in her eyes and said, "I guess I have no choice. I want *you* to be happy."

Love addiction is the paradox that Jennifer's situation describes—it is love out of balance, loving the other too much while loving the self too little. In addictive relationships, ego boundaries are weak or nonexistent. The love addict's attention is focused on the other rather than on the self.

The basis for a healthy relationship with another must be a healthy relationship with yourself. Without an adequate amount of self-love, you won't be able to have a healthy love relationship with another person. If you are a love addict, you learned early on to believe that you're unworthy and undeserving of love. The needs and desires of your beloved are always more important than your own. You've been conditioned to love in an unbalanced manner.

The diagram below illustrates the problem of love addiction:

Addictive Love Is

An Intense or Exaggerated

Reaction (to)   *Involvement* (with)   *Expectation (of)*

The Other

That Results In:

Inadequate

Attention   *Concern*   *Care*

For Yourself

Recovery from love addiction requires bringing love into balance—you must learn to develop a healthy regard for yourself.

The Addictive Relationship

In a healthy relationship, the basis for love of the other is self-love. Each partner feels a sense of wholeness and completeness. Each feels worthy and deserving of being loved. Each has, to some satisfactory degree, mastered the developmental tasks that are requisite for forming an intimate relationship. Each partner is able to focus on the here-and-now while having healthy expectations for what can develop in the future. The purpose of the relationship is mutual growth and fulfillment.

In an addictive relationship, there is not the same sense of wholeness or completeness within the partners. The love addict feels a sense of incompleteness, emptiness, despair, and sadness that he or she seeks to remedy by connecting with another. Developmental issues have not been satisfactorily resolved. The relationship is viewed as a means of meeting one's needs for love and security rather than as a shared experience.

The addictive relationship becomes an arena for trying to resolve unfinished business from the past. All behavior is directed toward making right in the present relationship what was unfulfilling or painful in the past. As Robin Norwood demonstrated in *Women Who Love Too Much*, love addicts attempt to fulfill their unsatisfied needs for love, affection, and nurturing in relationships that re-create the painful conditions of childhood. All the emotion and frustration of the present may refer exclusively to the past—and the love addict is, in this sense, "using" his or her partner as a director might use an actor in a play. No wonder the real issues of the present relationship have no chance of being worked out or even recognized!

Addictive relationships are characterized by a simultaneous excess and lack of love. An overabundance of love or obsessive attention is bestowed upon the other, while an inadequate amount is given to the self. If you are involved in an addictive relationship, your reactions to the other, involvement with the other, and expectations of the other are all excessive and overblown. You think and daydream about your partner much too often; you give excessively of your time, energy, and hopes. All healthy boundaries disappear in terms of what you are willing to do or to give up to maintain the relationship. You've given all your power away to the other. Your hopes for security and fulfillment depend on the other's love.

Addictive love is always given at the expense of self. When too much attention, concern, and care are given to the other, the self suffers. Ultimately, the self is abandoned in favor of the other. The chart below shows the typical imbalance that can result:

The Self	The Other
is emotionally over-available	is emotionally unavailable
focuses on the other	focuses on self
gives encouragement, support, money, time, and so on	has needs and desires met
gives more than 50 percent	gives less than 50 percent

gives up or loses power	gains power
validates the other	is validated
tolerates inappropriate behavior	often engages in inappropriate behavior
attaches or becomes enmeshed with the other	detaches or moves away from the other

The portrait that emerges is of a one-sided relationship in which one partner does most of the giving while the other receives. The giving partner is oriented toward the other. The roles and responses that the giving partner engages in have been learned early in life and must be unlearned if a healthy relationship is to be developed and maintained.

Love Addiction as a Learned Response

The love addict's behaviors are learned from two sources: the family and society in general. The family is the primary source for the development of your beliefs and attitudes about intimate relationships and the way you behave in relation to others. It was in the home environment of your childhood that you learned either to love and trust yourself or to feel helpless and dependent. Your family taught you to feel worthy and deserving of love (or to feel worthless and unlovable). As a child you experimented with ways to get your needs met for love and affection. If you grew up in a dysfunctional family where your needs for nurturing were *not* met, you no doubt developed erroneous beliefs about close relationships an learned unhealthy ways of trying to meet your needs.

Society is also a culprit in helping individuals to develop erroneous beliefs about relationships, and in teaching unhealthy relating behaviors. Our society emphasizes an external means of gaining satisfaction via money and material possessions. We are taught to look outside ourselves to feel complete and fulfilled. The media emphasizes how good we will feel with the right car, jeans, or sexy partner. Movies, television, and music reinforce the belief that the other has the power to determine our moods and our feelings about ourselves. Listen to any pop song and you'll hear the yearnings of one who needs the other in his or her life to feel good. Our society encourages us to be "other-oriented" and in so doing encourages addictive relationships.

The love-addicted individual, already needy and dependent, chooses an unrealistic and erroneous model when he or she relies on the media to teach relating behaviors. As a result of messages from an unhealthy or dysfunctional family environment, and from an externally oriented society, you form a false picture of what behaviors are necessary to achieve a feeling of well-being and to interact with others in close relationships. These pictures or messages are replayed and the behaviors are repeated in each unhealthy relationship. It's only when these erroneous messages and behaviors are examined and unlearned that healthy relationships can be developed.

What erroneous beliefs are learned from the dysfunctional family and from society?

- *I cannot trust the other to meet my needs.*
  If you grew up in a dysfunctional family, you more than likely did not have your needs for love and security met. As a result, you learned to reduce your

expectations; you came to believe that your partner would be inconsistent, unreliable, and unavailable.

- *I will be hurt by love.*
  If love was not easily shared in your home, or if you saw hurtful acts committed in the name of love, you came to assume that "love hurts." You feel that your relationships are destined to be chaotic, painful, and destructive. To love is to "meet your Waterloo."

- *I cannot be myself and be loved.*
  In dysfunctional families, feelings are denied. If you grew up in this type of family, you probably learned that you would be rejected if you expressed your true feelings. Most importantly, you learned that anger was not to be expressed.

- *I have no control over what happens to me.*
  Growing up in a chaotic environment, you probably believed that this was "the way it is"—that families operate this way and cannot be changed. You felt and feel *powerless*.

- *I do not deserve love.*
  Most significantly, you learned that you were not worthy of being loved. You grew up believing that you must earn the right to be loved. Related to this, you came to assume that you must be perfect if you are to be loved, and must assume all the responsibility for making things work.

- *I must look outside of myself to find happiness.*
  From society, you learned that external things are supposed to make you feel good about yourself. Everything from pop songs to perfume ads taught you that you must find another person to validate you, to make you feel whole and worthwhile.

Your unhealthy responses in your relationship are based on the above set of mistaken beliefs. Such beliefs prevent you from growing emotionally, from developing intimacy, and from interacting in healthy ways in a relationship. Until you change these beliefs, you'll continue to respond to your partner and the relationship in unhealthy, addictive ways.

The Love-Addictive Response

There are three major types of love-addictive responses in close relationships: 1)overreacting to the other or the relationship, 2) becoming excessively involved with the other and the relationship, 3) having unrealistic expectations of the other and the relationship. In this section, we will explore each of these modalities.

Overreacting

Love-addicted partners in a relationship often make mountains out of molehills. You overvalue your partner or the significance of the relationship, consistently placing your partner's welfare above your own. You overreact by giving excessive amounts of love and attention to your partner while denying appropriate care and attention to yourself. You give others the power to control your feelings and moods by overreacting to everything they do or say, even overreacting to what they fail to do or say!

Does your relationship seem imbued with life-altering potential? Are you inflating a simple process of getting to know someone better? Do you search desperately for a relationship? Do you stay in a bad relationship just to be involved? All of these behaviors indicate that you're reacting inappropriately.

How do you tell the difference between a normal reaction to someone who you think is pretty nice and an unhealthy overreaction? Ask yourself whether you:

- *Experience intense feelings of need for the other.*
  "I can't survive without Sue. I don't know what I'd do if we ever broke up."

- *Experience intense feelings of need for the relationship.*
  "I have to be involved. I don't feel complete unless there's a man in my life."

- *Experience intense feelings of infatuation.*
  "When I'm involved with someone, I'm in a continual state of excitement. Sometimes I can't eat or sleep."

- *Experience feelings of jealousy and possessiveness.*
  "I can't stand it when Fran talks to other men. If I could, I'd keep her all to myself."

- *Are self-sacrificing and self-depriving.*
  "No amount of money is too much to spend on the man I love."

- *Express affection prematurely.*
  (After going out with Mark once.) "I found this really cute card to send to Mark. I want to let him know how special he is to me."

- *Disclose your feelings prematurely.*
  (After dating John for a month.) "I wanted John to really get to know me, so I didn't hold anything back."

- *Blame yourself when conflict occurs.*
  "I know I shouldn't have asked Tom why he didn't call when he said he would. Everyone makes mistakes. Now he's mad at me."

- *Are unable to endure separation.*
  "Annie and I can't stand to be apart. When we're away from each other for too long, we end up feeling depressed."

Excessive Involvement

You are responding in an unhealthy or addictive manner when you have an all-consuming involvement with the other and the relationship. You are excessively involved when your life seems out of balance because all of your mental, physical, and emotional energy is directed toward the other. He or she is constantly in your thoughts, and you have ceased to have a life of your own.

You are intensely or overly involved when you:

- *Are preoccupied with the other and the relationship.*
  Joe always has Julie on his mind. Even when he's with the guys, part of him is thinking of her.

- *Have limited or no social life outside of the relationship.*
  Ann's life revolves around her relationship with Tony. She rarely sees her friends anymore. When she's not with Tony, she is fantasizing about seeing him.

- *Have no interests outside of the relationship.*
  Carrie no longer has her own interests or hobbies since she started dating Bob. She prefers to do the things that he likes.

- *Find that your life revolves around hearing from and seeing the other.*

Jodie waits by the phone for calls from Alan. She won't even leave the house or talk on the phone to friends when she's expecting a call from him.

- *You notice that every act or event is connected to some aspect of your partner.*
  Teresa can't talk about anything but Joe. No matter what the topic, she gets around to including him in the conversation. Her friends are growing weary of hearing about Joe.

- *Find that your life is out of balance.*
  Marilyn's life consists of seeing Steve and going to work. Everything that she does is either connected to making a living (because she has to) or her relationship with Steve.

Unrealistic Expectations

A relationship that is grounded more in fantasy than in reality is based on unrealistic expectations. You focus more on the future or the outcome of the relationship than on the here-and-now. When you won't give the relationship time to develop, you are also responding unrealistically. Such expectations are reflected in your attempts to control, manipulate, or change your partner so that the relationship will fit your fantasy of what a relationship should be. When you expect the relationship to meet your needs for basic self-esteem and security, then you are expecting too much.

You have unrealistic expectations for the relationship if you:

- *Focus only on the future and the outcome of the relationship.*
  Diane cannot enjoy the time she spends with Phil.

She is constantly worried about where the relationship will go.

- *Expect the relationship to change your life—to make your life better or make you feel better about yourself.*
  Stan just knows that when he meets the "right" woman he will be happy. He's content to simply go through the motions of living until she comes along.

- *Play roles, engage in ritualized activities, and "act out the fantasy."*
  Doreen expects a relationship to operate the way she sees relationships operating in the movies. She acts "the way you are supposed to act when you are in love." Her true feelings don't matter.

- *Attempt to change the other to fit the fantasy.*
  There are a lot of things that Ann doesn't like about Tim. In fact, she doesn't really feel that he's the best person for her, but she thinks that she can turn him into her "dream guy" with enough love and effort. She spends all her time wishing, hoping, and trying to change Tim.

Love-addictive responses are unhealthy ways of interacting in a relationship. They actually hinder rather than promote the development of a close and lasting bond. To establish and maintain a healthy and mutually satisfying relationship, you must be able to unlearn these unhealthy response patterns and replace them with appropriate and healthy behaviors.

Further Reading

Halpern, Howard M. *How to Break Your Addiction to a Person.* New York: McGraw Hill, 1982.

Norwood, Robin. *Women Who Love Too Much.* Los Angeles: Jeremy P. Taracher, 1985.

Subby, Robert. *Lost in the Shuffle: The Co-dependent Reality.* Deerfield Beach, FL: Health Communications, Inc. 1987.

Woititz, Janet G. *Struggle for Intimacy.* Deerfield Beach, FL: Health Communications, Inc. 1985.

2

Cognitive-Behavioral Therapy and Recovery From Love Addiction

Mary and Bob have been dating for three months. They've gone out every weekend since they began dating. Bob usually calls before 9:00 p.m. on Thursday to confirm the weekend plans. It's Thursday night, 10:00, and Bob hasn't called. Here's a schedule of Mary's reactions to this event:

10:15 p.m. Mary has taken a seat between the phone and the clock. Each time she looks at the clock she thinks:

"This is crazy."
"Something is wrong."
"I did something wrong."
"I won't hear from him."
"He's seeing someone else."

The more Mary thinks about Bob not calling, the more upset she becomes. She lifts the receiver to make sure that the phone is working properly.

11:00 p.m. Mary's anxiety has begun to take an angry turn.

"That turkey!"
"It's not fair."
"I trusted him."
"I'll show him."
"I'm going to tell him off."
"I'm not going to answer the phone tomorrow."

11:30 p.m.

"It's getting late."
"He won't call now."
"He may never call me again."

12:00 p.m. Mary has become depressed. She decides to go to bed, but tosses and turns all night.

4:00 a.m. Mary awakens with Bob on her mind.

"He didn't call."
"Why didn't he call?"
"Something is wrong."
"I've got to hear from him."
"I'll call him at work."

7:00 a.m. Mary again awakens with Bob on her mind. She is tired from not getting enough rest.

"I really like Bob."
"I hope I see him again."
"There's no one like him."
"What happened?"
"I feel terrible."

7:30 a.m. Mary feels awful. She's weak, tired, and depressed. She can't drag herself from bed. She calls in sick to work and spends the day in bed.

Cognitive-Behavioral Theory

If the episode with Mary were explained in cognitive-behavioral terms, it would be said that Mary's thoughts shaped both her emotions and her behavior. It was not Bob's failure to call that caused Mary to sink into depression, but rather her negative thoughts and conclusions about not receiving a call. Mary's thoughts have managed to trigger a range of emotions in her, from fear to anger. Ultimately her thoughts influenced her to call in sick to work and to spend the day with the covers pulled over her head.

In cognitive-behavioral terms, Mary's negative thought patterns caused her to experience emotional upheaval and to engage in unhealthy behavior. According to Dobson (1988), all cognitive-behavioral approaches share three fundamental concepts:

1. *Cognitive activity (thinking) affects behavior.* When you experience an event, you think about it. It is your thoughts about the event that will affect your response to it. Your perception of the event can affect your emotions and actions in either a positive or negative manner.

2. *Cognitive activity may be monitored and altered.* It's possible for you to know and assess your thought patterns. This awareness can help you change the way in which you think about or perceive events.

3. *Desired behavioral change may be affected by changing thought patterns.* If you can learn to change your

thought patterns, then you can change your behavior.

Automatic Thoughts, Anticipation, Self-Monitoring

There are three key concepts in cognitive-behavioral approaches that are especially useful in understanding and treating love addiction:

1. *Automatic thoughts.* According to Beck (1976), we are constantly communicating with ourselves as we interpret events, monitor our behavior, and make predictions and generalizations. This communication takes place through "automatic thoughts."

   Automatic thoughts have characteristics that are readily seen in love-addictive thought patterns. Automatic thoughts are:

   - *Specific and discrete.* They usually occur in a shorthand or telegraphic style.

   - *Autonomous.* They can arise without deliberation, reasoning, or reflection. They take no effort to initiate and occur almost by reflex—they "just happen."

   - *Plausible or reasonable.* They are accepted as valid even though we don't question or test their logic. They can occur despite the fact that they are contrary to objective evidence.

   - *Repetitive and powerful.* They can be of an obsessive nature; they are difficult to "turn off."

   - *Idiosyncratic.* They can stimulate a certain set of reactions as determined by the situation.

2. *Anticipation.* The meaning of your experiences is determined by your expectations of consequences. Your emotions and behavior can be changed by your expectations. Your expectations are based upon what you feel will occur as a result of your belief system. If you've developed an erroneous belief system, then you will have inappropriate expectations for your experiences.

3. *Self-monitoring of behavior.* Part of the internal communicating that you do with yourself consists of monitoring your behavior. You monitor your thoughts, feelings, and actions. You also look at your options and make decisions. This self-monitoring can lead to maladaptive reactions, however. You can either over- or undermonitor your behavior. If you overmonitor your behavior, you become self-conscious and perhaps even unable to act. If you undermonitor your thoughts and impulses, you may disregard the consequences of your behavior. Much of the unhealthy behavior seen as love-addictive responses occurs because of a self-monitoring deficit.

The cognitive-behavioral approach assumes that reflection occurs after an event, and that this reflection may affect behavioral change. The approach also assumes that the individual can set goals and change his or her behavior to achieve higher levels of health and functioning.

The basic goals of cognitive-behavioral approaches are to have the individual:

• Become aware of thoughts

• Identify inaccurate thoughts

• Replace inaccurate thoughts with accurate ones

- Reinforce accurate thought patterns through behavioral tasks

How can you use cognitive-behavioral goals to facilitate your recovery from love addiction?

Cognitive-Behavioral Strategies

Love addiction is characterized by maladaptive or unhealthy responses to your partner and the relationship as a result of learning erroneous ways of interacting in close relationships. These erroneous belief systems condition you to appraise or perceive events related to the relationship in erroneous or unhealthy ways. Your thoughts about an event or situation negatively affect your emotions and actions.

Here is what happened to Mary, expressed in cognitive-behavioral terms:

Event	Thoughts	Beliefs
No call from Bob by 9:00.	"Something is wrong." "I did something wrong."	"I will be abandoned." "I can expect to be hurt."

Feelings	Actions
Fear, anxiety, depression.	Mary called in sick and stayed in bed.

Event: Bob did not call by a certain hour.

Thoughts: Mary perceived the event to be terrible and thought about it in these terms.

Beliefs: Mary's thoughts about the event were influenced by her erroneous beliefs about relationships.

Feelings: Mary's thoughts triggered a number of emotions, from fear to anger.

Actions: Mary became depressed and was unable to leave her bed.

Mary's Automatic Thoughts

Mary experienced a series of "automatic thoughts" when she did not receive a call from Bob. These are the characteristics of automatic thoughts as they relate to Mary:

- *Specific and discrete.* Mary thought such things as: "This is crazy," and "Something is wrong."

- *Autonomous.* Mary's thoughts occurred by reflex. They just started to "pop into her head."

- *Plausible and reasonable.* Mary's conditioning had taught her to expect to be hurt in a relationship. It only made sense that something would go wrong. It never occurred to Mary that there may have been a legitimate reason why Bob didn't call.

- *Repetitious and powerful.* Once the negative thoughts started, Mary couldn't stop them. Each thought triggered another thought that eventually brought Mary to the point of depression.

- *Idiosyncratic.* Mary's experiences in her family, and the messages that she has received from society, have conditioned her to engage in a specific set of thought patterns when certain events occur within a close relationship. Thus Bob's failure to call fulfilled her expectations about being hurt and abandoned.

Mary's Anticipation

Mary has learned to expect the worst from a relationship. She expects to be hurt by her partner, and she expects to be abandoned at some point in the relationship. Her belief system has shaped her expectations of the consequences of the event. Since Mary already has a negative set of expectations for close relationships, her reactions can be anticipated. Mary's emotions and actions are related to her "relationship expectations."

Mary's Self-Monitoring of Behavior

Mary suffers from an undermonitoring deficit. She's unable to see how her thoughts or actions affect her emotions. Despite the negative consequences of these behaviors, she engaged in watching the clock, checking the phone, calling in sick, and staying in bed. She was unable to see that these behaviors only worsened her bad feelings and led her deeper into depression.

Cognitive-Behavioral Strategies for Mary

Cognitive-behavioral strategies can help Mary monitor her thoughts and behavior. She can learn to use these strategies to change her behavior so that she can respond in healthier ways in a relationship. Below is an example of how Mary can work to change her addictive responses to healthier ways of thinking and behaving:

1. *Become aware of thoughts.* Mary has to recall the thoughts that came to mind as she waited for Bob's call.

"Wonder what he's doing?"
"Ring, phone!"
"Come on, Bob, call me."
"It's late."
"He should have called by now."

Mary was experiencing automatic thoughts of a negative nature even before the appointed hour for Bob's call.

2. *Identify inaccurate thoughts.* Any thought that is based on an erroneous belief system or has not been proven to be true can be considered to be inaccurate.

   Inaccurate thoughts at 10:15 p.m.:

   "This is crazy."
   "Something is wrong."
   "I did something wrong."
   "I won't hear from him."
   "He's seeing someone else."

3. *Replace inaccurate thoughts with accurate ones.* (Bob has been consistent in his behavior toward Mary. Had Bob broken dates or frequently not called as he said he would, then another set of "accurate thoughts" would be appropriate.)

   Change "This is crazy" to "This is disappointing."

   Change "Something is wrong" to "There's a reason why Bob hasn't called."

   Change "I did something wrong" to "Bob has a good reason for not calling."

   Change "I won't hear from him" to "He may not be able to call me tonight."

Change "He's seeing someone else" to " I know Bob likes me, so I expect to hear from him."

4. *Reinforce accurate thought patterns through behavioral tasks.* Mary could engage in any number of more appropriate activities, such as reading, taking a bubble bath, watching TV, doing her nails, doing household chores. What she should *not* do is watch the clock or the phone.

Conclusions

Recovery from love addiction begins with an understanding of the power of your thoughts. You must 1) become aware of the erroneous beliefs under which you are operating, 2) become aware of your "automatic thoughts," 3) challenge these thoughts, and 4) change your thoughts so that you can change your behavior.

The recovery strategies suggested in this book are based on cognitive-behavioral approaches. Each section describing strategies begins with exercises to help you change your thought patterns. *Developing Healthy Reactions* requires you to change your other-enhancing thoughts to self-enhancing thoughts. In *Developing Healthy Involvement,* you'll change other-focused thoughts to self-focused thoughts. In *Developing Healthy Expectations,* you'll focus on thoughts of changing the self rather than those related to changing the other. The chapters that follow each thought-change chapter contain exercises to help you change your behaviors.

When you learn to change your thoughts and beliefs, the battle is half won. In learning to change them, you'll free yourself to feel and act in healthier ways. When you can think, feel, and act in healthy and appropriate ways, you're ready to develop the type of healthy, loving, and lasting relationship that you've always desired.

Further Reading

Beck, Aaron T. *Cognitive Therapy and the Emotional Disorders.* New York: International Universities Press, 1976.

Dobson, Keith S. *Handbook of Cognitive-Behavioral Therapies.* London: Guiford Press, 1988.

McKay, Matthew, et al. *Thoughts and Feelings: The Art of Cognitive Stress Intervention.* Oakland, CA: New Harbinger Publications, Inc., 1981.

3

Assessing Addictive Thoughts and Behaviors

Addictive thought patterns are learned early in life and reinforced over many years. Unhealthy ways of thinking and responding become habits. You may consider some of your addictive responses to be "typical" in close relationships. You may feel that loving the other means continuously having the other on your mind. You may assume that there is something wrong or at least un-romantic about a relationship in which each partner has his or her own interests and friends. You may even feel that others who develop loving and lasting relationships are just "lucky" enough to find the "right" person. You might also have a gnawing feeling that something isn't right in the way you respond in relationships, because yours never seem to turn out in the way you desire.

Before you can make changes in your close relation-ships, you must become aware of your unhealthy thought patterns and behaviors. You must learn to distinguish addictive patterns of thinking and behavior from healthy ways of responding in a relationship.

This chapter contains two inventories for you to complete. The first, the Inventory of Addictive Thoughts and Behaviors (IATB), is designed to assess your thought patterns and behaviors as they relate to each of the addictive responses. After completing and scoring the IATB, you'll discover the areas (Reactions, Involvement, Expectations) that will require the greatest amount of work on your part. You may have to work equally hard to make changes in all areas.

Begin the change process by setting goals for each of the addictive response areas. For instance, if you're in a new relationship and your response to an inventory item indicates that you often send cards or give gifts prematurely, you may set a goal for resisting the temptation to repeat this behavior too soon. Use your responses to the inventory to help you decide where to begin the change process. After a while, retake the inventory and evaluate your progress.

The second inventory, Relationship Analysis, will help you identify unhealthy patterns in your relationships. It may be helpful to write your responses to this inventory in journal form. The instructions suggest that you think about your relationships within the past five years. You may find it even more helpful, however, to recall *all* of the significant relationships in which you've been involved during your lifetime. Take your time in completing this inventory—think each relationship through carefully. The more thorough you are, the better. You'll find that patterns will emerge. You'll notice similar traits in the individuals to whom you are attracted. You may find that each of your relationships begins and ends in the same way. These unhealthy patterns must be identified if you are to change them. And they must be changed if you are to develop and maintain the healthy relationships you desire.

Inventory of Addictive Thoughts and Behaviors (IATB)

Certain thought patterns and behaviors occur repeatedly in addictive relationships. Think about your current or most recent relationship. What did you feel and how did you react in the relationship? Rate the following thoughts and behaviors according to the degree to which you agree or disagree that they occurred in your relationship. Use the following scale:

1 = Strongly Agree
2 = Agree
3 = Disagree
4 = Strongly Disagree

___2___ 1. I knew right away the he/she was "the one."
___1___ 2. I think of him/her all of the time.
___1___ 3. I can't stand not knowing where I stand with him/her.
___1___ 4. I find it hard to concentrate, read, watch TV, or anything when I'm not with him/her.
___2___ 5. I am miserable when I'm not with him/her.
___2___ 6. I cancel plans with my friends to be with him/her.
___1___ 7. I feel better about myself when I'm in a relationship.
___1___ 8. I tend to drop hobbies, interests, and so on when I become involved in a relationship.
___4___ 9. When I'm not in a relationship, I'm looking for one.
___2___ 10. I won't leave the house when I think he/she will call.
___2___ 11. I test him/her to see how much I am cared for or loved.
___2___ 12. I make all of my plans with him/her in mind.

_2_ 13. I want to know that he/she is "mine."

_2_ 14. I keep track of my telephone conversations and dates with him/her.

_4_ 15. I try to change qualities that I find unacceptable in him/her.

_1_ 16. I am usually the person in the relationship who gives the gifts, surprises, and so on.

_1_ 17. I spend a lot of time analyzing his/her words and actions.

_1_ 18. I spend a lot of time fantasizing about our future together.

_1_ 19. I don't believe in holding anything back (keeping anything private) from my partner.

_2_ 20. I talk about him/her all of the time to my friends.

_3_ 21. I don't plan to make any major changes or carry out any major plans in my life until I meet the "right" person.

_3_ 22. I usually feel it is my fault when something goes wrong in the relationship.

_2_ 23. I replay our last date or conversation over and over in my mind.

_1_ 24. I find myself hoping and waiting for things to get better in my relationship.

_1_ 25. I am the one who provides most of the support and encouragement in the relationship.

_4_ 26. I memorize his/her license plate.

_1_ 27. I fear he/she will be attracted to someone else.

_1_ 28. I become excited or anxious when I expect to see or hear from him/her.

Scoring: Review your scores of 1 and 2 (Strongly Agree and Agree). The following item numbers represent addictive thoughts and behaviors related to Reactions, Involvement, and Expectations.

Reactions: 1, 5, 9, 13, 16, 19, 22, 25, 27, and 28
Involvement: 2, 4, 6, 8, 10, 12, 14, 17, 20, 23, and 26
Expectations: 3, 7, 11, 15, 18, 21, and 24
Reactions _____

_____

_____

_____

Now that you have completed the survey, list the thoughts and/or behaviors in which you typically engage.

_____

_____

_____

_____

What patterns do you see?

_____

_____

_____

_____

Relationship Analysis

Analyzing your relationships can be helpful in identifying unhealthy behavioral patterns. Look for similarities in individuals to whom you are attracted. These similar traits often trigger unhealthy behaviors. Think about your relationships over the last five years and answer the following questions for each relationship. (You may want to make photocopies of this and the following page.)

1. Name:

2. Most striking physical feature(s):

3. Most striking personality feature(s):

4. First impressions (first meeting):

5. Feelings at the beginning of the relationship:

6. Who initiated the relationship?

7. What initially attracted you to him/her?

8. How did the relationship start?

9. Who was the pursuer?

10. How did you spend time in the relationship?

11. Who made the decisions (who was more dominant)?

12. What was the emotional tone of the relationship?

13. Were your needs (emotional/sexual) satisfied in the relationship?

14. How long did the relationship last?

15. Who ended the relationship?

16. How did the relationship end?

17. Why did the relationship end?

18. What were your feelings at the end of the relation-ship?

19. What do you most remember about him/her and the relationship?

20. How was this relationship similar to your previous relationships?

Reactions:_____

_____

_____

_____

When you become aware of some of the thinking pat-terns and behaviors that prevent you from responding to your partner in a healthy manner, you can begin the process of change. But first you must *choose* to change.

4

Choosing to Change

Making and then following through on the decision to change is often the most difficult aspect of recovery. You may know that you are involved in a destructive relationship, but for some reason you just can't seem to let it go. You may realize that you engage in the same behaviors time and time again, but you just can't seem to change your way of responding. You may feel that your self-respect is slowly being eroded, but you can't seem to do things differently. You may even have tried to change on several occasions, but somehow couldn't stick with your decision. Change has been a bridge that you've been unable to cross.

This chapter is about crossing that bridge. What does change mean, what does it require, how do you effect it, what obstacles can you expect, and how will you feel once you've experienced some success with the process? While change is always a little difficult initially, it can be an exciting, challenging, and rewarding venture.

Just what are you in for when you decide to change? What exactly does choosing to change mean? Change is:

- *Taking a risk.* When you decide to make changes in the way you think, feel, and act in your relationship, you're taking a risk. When *you* change, your relationship will most certainly change as well; your relationship may also end. If you've always been the "giver" in your relationship, and you begin to ask for what you need, your partner may resist. He or she may find the changed "you" perplexing, or even irritating. Your changed self may be so distasteful to your partner that he or she will choose to leave the relationship. As frightening as this risk may seem, having your relationship end is a possibility that you must consider when you decide to change.

- *Facing the unknown.* As painful as your addiction may be, you know what to expect. You listen to the same tapes each time. The same play is reenacted in each new relationship. You choose familiar actors (similar to the significant others in your earlier life) and you play out the same parts with the same results. You can expect to yearn, to give away power, and to hurt. But at least you know what to expect. You won't know what to expect when you decide to change the way you relate to your partner. Things will certainly be different, but you don't know *how* different. You don't know how either of you will respond. The only answer is to trust that you will be able to handle whatever the situation brings.

- *Change.* Changing means doing things differently, thinking about yourself in new and positive ways. You must be determined not to repeat the same old patterns that bring the same unsatisfactory results. To change means to act like a healthy person even when you don't feel like one, to adopt new ways of thinking and behaving. Change involves "trying out a new tape."

- *Making things happen.* You must take responsibility for making good things happen in your relationship and your life. Your partner *will not* change for you—no amount of hoping, wishing, or manipulating can make your partner change for you. You and *only you* can change the ways in which you respond in your relationship. In changing, you are actively involved in creating the relationship that you desire (or in walking away from a relationship that cannot meet your needs).

- *Discovering your personal power.* When you make even the smallest premeditated change, you feel better about yourself. You feel a new sense of self-confidence, self-reliance, and self-respect. You realize that you really can "handle" your relationships. When you change, you begin to discover your power. You have the capability and the power to determine what happens in your relationships and your life. You begin to understand that you no longer have to be a victim or a martyr in your relationships. You discover that you don't have to accept "crumbs," nor do you have to give 110 percent to make a relationship work. You realize that you too can ask to have your needs met. When your needs are not met (which can be the case sometimes), you will see that you really do have the power to say "no, thank you" and move on so that you can make yourself available for a healthier relationship. Change is never easy. It requires commitment and hard work. In order to change, you must:

- *Accept yourself, addiction and all.* You are who you are. Yes, you may not be very happy with yourself for "loving too much," but for now that's a reality for you. You are still worthy and deserving of love and respect from yourself (first of all) and from others. Most importantly, you must accept and approve of your desire to change and grow.

- *Confront the unhealthy aspects of your behavior.* To change, you must become aware of the ways in which you are thinking and behaving in unhealthy ways. You must be willing to unlearn these unhealthy patterns and relearn healthier ways of thinking and behaving.

- *Assume responsibility for your self-worth.* Another person can only temporarily make you feel good about yourself. When he or she withdraws the attention and love, those good feelings they created in you will go, too. In choosing to change, you give up the idea that you're dependent on someone else for your good feelings about yourself. When you decide to make changes in your relationship, you are choosing to take responsibility for making yourself feel worthy and deserving of love.

Steps to Change

The change process consists of five steps. Each step in the process is necessary and important. With each step, you will come closer to being the healthy partner that you wish to be in a relationship.

Step 1: *Determine why you are choosing to change.* Ask

yourself why it's necessary or desirable for you to change the way in which you respond in your relationships.

Step 2: *Choose to change.* Make a conscious decision to change the way in which you're responding in your relationships. In choosing to change, you are acknowledging your responsibility for the process. Write a contract.

Step 3: *Decide what you would like to change.* Set goals for change. Decide what changes you can comfortably make. Start small, then move on to more significant changes.

Step 4: *Start some aspect of the change process now.* Begin with some of the less threatening changes (less threatening, that is, to you and your partner). You *do not* have to leave the relationship unless you determine later that leaving is your best option.

Step 5: *Evaluate your progress and reward yourself for taking steps toward change.* Pat yourself on the back for even the smallest effort. You'll feel good about yourself, knowing that *you're* capable of making things happen in your relationship.

Step 1: Determine Why You Are Choosing to Change

Think about the reasons why you wish to change the way you interact in close relationships. Consider how you feel about yourself as a result of being in your current relationship. List your reasons below.

I am choosing to change because:

1.

2.

3.

4.

5.

6.

7.

8.

9.

10.

Step 2: Choose to Change

Complete the following contract and post it someplace conspicuous.

I,_____, choose to change my unhealthy thoughts and behaviors to healthy ones, so that I can develop and maintain a healthy, loving, and lasting relationship. I commit myself to all the necessary work to refute my erroneous beliefs, correct my inaccurate thoughts, and change my unhealthy behaviors.

Step 3: Decide What You Would Like to Change

Set goals. Review your responses to the Inventory of Addictive Thoughts and Behaviors. For each area (Reactions, Involvement, Expectations), choose thoughts or behaviors that you would like to change (use items that scored 1 or 2).

Goals for Developing Healthy Reactions

1.

2.

3.

Goals for Developing Healthy Involvement

1.

2.

3.

Goals for Developing Healthy Expectations

1.

2.

3.

Step 4: Start Some Aspect of the Change Process Now

Below write goals from Step 3 that you will begin to work toward now.

1.

2.

3.

Step 5: Evaluate Your Progress and Reward Your Success

Goal:

Reaction:

Reward:

Goal:

Reaction:

Reward:

Goal:

Reaction:

Reward:

Goal:

Reaction:

Reward:

Goal:

Reaction:

Reward:

Goal:

Reaction:

Reward:

My Reward:_____

_____

_____

Example

Betty and Ron have dated for almost two years. During this time, they have experienced a "push-and-pull" relationship. Ron pushes Betty for closeness. He calls every day, wants to see her as often as possible, and is jealous of any attention she receives from other men. He insists on talking about "their future," but in vague terms. As soon as Betty begins to feel close and wants to make the relationship work, Ron pulls away. He mentions that his financial situation isn't good—rather than spending so much time having fun, he needs to concentrate on his career. At this point, he often sees other women and leaves clues so that Betty will find out. Ron pulls away until Betty becomes angry and says she won't see him. Each time a push-and-pull episode occurs, Betty stops seeing Ron for a while (a week was the longest period), but soon relents, and the process starts all over again. Ron then becomes the perfect partner for a month or so. Betty has started to notice that she is always in crisis in this relationship. She is tired of the emotional roller coaster on which she interacts with Ron. Here are Betty's responses to the exercises in the change process.

Step 1: *I choose to change because:*

> 1. *I don't feel good about myself.*
>
> 2. *My needs are not being met.*
>
> 3. *I feel used.*
>
> 4. *I feel there is no future in this relationship.*
>
> 5. *I feel that I deserve better.*
>
> 6. *I don't feel that things will change.*

Step 2: *Choose to change.* Complete the following contract:

I, *Betty,* choose to change my unhealthy responses to healthy thoughts and behaviors so that I can develop and maintain a healthy, loving, and lasting relationship. I commit myself to all the necessary work to refute my erroneous beliefs, correct my inaccurate thoughts, and change my unhealthy behaviors.

Step 3: *Decide what you would like to change.* Set goals.

Goals for Developing Healthy Reactions

1. *Stop thinking that Ron is the "only" man for me. (#1)*

2. *Desire rather than need Ron. (#5)*

3. *Stop needing Ron to "belong" to me. (#13)*

Goals for Developing Healthy Involvement

1. *Think of Ron less. (#2)*

2. *Relax, let go, stop keeping track of calls, dates. (#14)*

3. *Take up some of my interests again. (#8)*

Goals for Developing Healthy Expectations

1. *Feel good about myself in or out of a relationship. (#7)*

2. *Concentrate on now; think/dream less about future. (#18)*

3. *Stop putting my life on hold. (#21)*

Step 4: *Start some aspect of the change process now.*

1. *Thinking of Ron less—myself more.*

2. *Stop keeping track of calls, dates.*

3. *Start working out at spa again.*

Step 5: *Evaluate your progress and reward your success.*

Goal: *Thinking of Ron less.*

Reaction: *The mental attachment exercises have been very helpful. I am focusing on myself more now.*

Reward: *Tell myself at least ten times a day how well I'm doing.*

Goal: *Stop keeping track of calls, dates.*

Reaction: *This was easier than I thought; I just simply refused to "take notes" any longer.*

Reward: *I'll treat myself to a good movie.*

Goal: *Take up my interests.*

Reaction: *Have been going to the spa on a regular basis. Also have gotten back into photography.*

Reward: *I deserve something special. I'm going to buy myself a new outfit.*

Goal:

Reaction:

Reward:

Goal:

Reaction:

Reward:

Goal:

Reaction:

Reward:

My Reward: *I'm real pleased with myself. Plan to take a long weekend soon with a couple of friends.*

Obstacles to Change

Change is never easy. It takes real determination and a lot of hard work. Change requires your commitment to stick with the process despite the obstacles you may face. The most common obstacles are:

- *Lack of readiness.* You may think that you want to change, but are not really ready. You may simply not hurt enough. You may not feel strong enough to follow through with the process. When you can physically, mentally, and emotionally no longer tolerate an unhealthy relationship, you *will* change.

  "I want to get out of the relationship. I know that it isn't good for me. I'm unhappy most of the time. I just can't leave now. I know that one day soon I will be strong enough to leave."

- *Fear.* The greatest obstacle to change is fear. Fear of losing the other, fear of being alone, fear of being lonely can prevent you from leaving an unhealthy situation. The fear that you cannot survive without a relationship (even a destructive one) will often make you hold on long after it is time to go.

  "I can't face being without her. I don't even want to think about what my life would be like."

- *Fantasies.* Fantasies about what will eventually happen in a relationship can keep you hanging on, waiting, and hoping for years. Because your partner keeps making promises about how wonderful the future will be (never mind all the pain you're going through now!), you stay—even though you're hurting, you stay.

"I know things will be different as soon as he gets his life together. He says he's going to leave his wife as soon as he gets a better job."

- *Lack of discipline.* You may have tried to change. You may have tried not sitting next to the phone, but somehow your change in behavior only lasted one day. You may have even tried to leave an unhealthy relationship for a short period of time. Whatever the case, you couldn't do what was necessary to follow through on your decision.

"I really tried not thinking of him all the time. I tried substituting thoughts about myself and my goals for thoughts of him. It was awfully hard to do, so I stopped after a couple of days."

Some Thoughts on Change

- Always remember that you only need to be ready for some aspect of change: you don't need to go the entire distance in a day.

- Realize that you will often be afraid to change a particular way of behaving. Only fear that is faced can lose its power. Facing your fears will give you a greater sense of your own power.

- Try to keep a clear head. Separate fantasy from reality. It's true that actions speak louder than words. If you stop short of taking action because your partner convinces you that things will soon change, set deadlines for seeing some tangible results.

- Don't expect change to come without work—it requires determination and self-discipline. This may all seem very difficult when you begin the process, but consciously made statements will eventually become internalized and uncomfortable actions will soon become habits.

- Reading this book will not in itself make you change. Change is action. *You* make change happen.

- Once you've crossed the bridge of change, you will not want to return to unhealthy ways of thinking and behaving. The payoff will be too rewarding— you may well wonder why you didn't change sooner.

Further Reading

Rush, Tom and Read, Randy. *I Want To Change But I Don't Know How.* Los Angeles: Price, Stern, Sloan. 1986.

5

Changing Addictive Thought Patterns: Enhancing the Self

I remember the first time I saw Jeff—he was the most handsome man I had ever seen. He also happened to be 'Mr. Eligible.' He had all the trappings of success—a great job, a condo, a sports-car. A friend introduced us and from then the relationship went zoom. I couldn't believe that Jeff really wanted to date me—I'm okay, but nothing special. I mean—I'm not the type of woman I thought Jeff would date—he's such a special guy. Boy, was he a charmer. He made me feel like I've never felt before. He made me—yes, me—feel beautiful. He adored my eyes, my figure, everything about me. When I was with him, I felt really important—he made me so happy. My whole life changed when I started dating Jeff. I felt alive. My usually dull life became exciting. Then he left. My life has gone downhill ever since.

Excessively enhancing your partner or the relationship is called overreacting. This happens when you idealize your partner, attributing qualities to him or her that he or she may not actually possess. In overreacting, you overvalue the other person, making him or her and the relationship more important in your life than is necessary or healthy.

In overreacting to your partner, you elevate him or her to a position of power. You give to this person the power to control your emotions and behaviors. You give the other the power to determine how you feel about yourself. If the other says you are beautiful, you feel beautiful. If the other wants to be with you, you feel desirable. If the other loves you, you feel worthy of love. You want and allow the other to validate you as a person.

The only problem in letting another person validate you and determine how you feel about yourself is that if he or she leaves, as Jeff did, your sense of validation leaves you as well. You are left feeling unwanted, unloved, and unworthy. When you seek from your partner and from a relationship what you should be providing for yourself, you are overreacting. In excessively enhancing your partner, you are giving away power that should be yours alone.

Overreaction is reinforced by obsessive thinking about your partner and the relationship. When you constantly connect your good feelings about yourself to another person, you are reinforcing the erroneous belief that you must seek love outside of yourself. You mistakenly believe that someone else has the power to control how you feel about yourself. Overreaction is a learned response. Early in your life you learned (erroneously) that you were not worthy or deserving of love. Because your needs for nurturing were not satisfied, you learned to "need" love—and that the person who provided that most precious commodity was crucial to your well-being. You probably learned that love must be earned, and that it is earned by focusing your attention, concern, and affection on the valued other rather than on yourself.

Learning to give as much mental attention to your own positive attributes as those of your partner is essential for a healthy relationship. In this chapter, you will learn how to change your focus from thoughts that enhance your partner to thoughts that enhance yourself. You'll learn to view yourself as the beautiful, lovable, capable, and powerful person you are.

Self-Enhancing Thought Patterns

Enhancing yourself is a matter of increasing your belief in your value, attractiveness, and desirability. It involves viewing yourself in the same flattering way you view your partner. To bring this about, you must consciously decide to think as highly of yourself as you do your partner. Learn to appreciate your own value!

To relate to your partner in a healthy manner, you must reject unhealthy reaction patterns and adopt healthier ones. Learning to develop self-enhancing thought patterns is the first step in developing healthy ways of relating.

Six steps are involved in the process of developing self-enhancing thoughts. Again, each step is essential to the process. Initially, some of the exercises as outlined in the six steps will feel uncomfortable to you. You may even feel phony repeating some of the statements. It's important to practice with self-discipline and complete the exercises no matter how uncomfortable they may feel initially. Soon you'll notice that you can engage in self-enhancing thoughts much more easily. Thinking positively about yourself will soon start to feel better. Eventually, it will feel quite natural. This is the goal of the process—to help you think of yourself as a valuable, attractive, and desirable individual who is worthy and deserving of love.

Step 1: *Gain an awareness of your perceptions about yourself and the other.* In this step you will identify your beliefs about yourself and your partner.

Step 2: *Gain an awareness of your inaccurate thoughts.* In this step, you will discover which inaccurate thoughts reinforce the enhancement of your partner at your own expense.

Step 3: *Choose to change unhealthy reactions to healthy ones.* Here you will set goals for increasing the number of self-enhancing thoughts that you experience.

Step 4: *Release unhealthy reactions.* In this step you will refute erroneous beliefs and correct inaccurate thoughts.

Step 5: *Learn and practice healthy reactions.* Here you repeat statements that reinforce healthy reactions, thoughts, feelings, and behaviors.

Step 6: *Evaluate your progress and reward your successes.* In this step you become aware of how your thought patterns are changing.

Step 1: Gaining an Awareness of Your Perceptions About Yourself and the Other

In the spaces below, list qualities or attributes that you feel best describe yourself and the other.

I am: *He/She is:*

1.   1.

2.   2.

3.   3.

4.   4.

5.   5.

6.   6.

7.   7.

8.   8.

9.   9.

10.   10.

What are your perceptions (in general) about yourself?

_____

_____

What are your perceptions (in general) about your partner?_____

_____

_____

How do your perceptions about yourself and your partner compare? (Do you perceive one of you to be more
acceptable, desirable, or attractive than the other?) _____

_____

_____

_____

How accurate are these perceptions? _____

_____

_____

_____

Example

Fran always ends up adoring and idolizing the man she dates. She starts out feeling what she calls "pretty cool" until she begins to like him. Then (as with Jeff) he becomes the most important thing in her life. According to Fran, "When I think about it, I don't really feel like I'm anybody until I have a man in my life. Just the fact that he "makes me his" means that I'm worthwhile. For him to want to spend time with me, and introduce me to his friends, says that I'm acceptable, I'm okay. It means he's proud of me; he approves of me. It gets to the point where I need that connection with him to feel okay. But it's a double-edged sword—the better he makes me feel by being with me, the more anxious I become that I'll lose him. Then I'll be a nobody again." Fran wants to break this cycle of infatuation and fear. She's working on changing patterns of reacting in her relationships. Here are Fran's responses to the awareness exercise:

I am:	*He/She is:*
1. *intelligent*	1. *handsome*
2. *a hard worker*	2. *intelligent*
3. *a good listener*	3. *financially secure*
4. *a good friend*	4. *ambitious*
5. *a good cook*	5. *sociable*
6. *shy*	6. *outgoing*
7.	7. *witty*
8.	8. *charming*
9.	9. *well-liked*
10.	10. *well-connected*

What are your perceptions (in general) about yourself? _I'm okay. Basically I'm a giver._

What are your perceptions about your partner? _When I look at his list, he's great. He has a lot going for him._

How do the perceptions about yourself and your partner compare? (Do you perceive one of you to be more accept-able, desirable, or attractive than the other?) _I guess I perceive Jeff to be more desirable than I am. Everything I listed about him is so positive. I just listed "Okay" qualities for myself._

How accurate are these perceptions? _Jeff really does have a lot going for him. This exercise is a real eye-opener—I guess I don't think much of myself._

Step 2: Gaining an Awareness of Your Inaccurate Thoughts

Below are five inaccurate thoughts that can lead to overreacting to your partner or a relationship. Read each thought. Then write your reaction to the thought in the space provided. As you read each thought, ask yourself: How do my feelings and behaviors reflect this thought pattern? React to each thought separately.

Inaccurate Thought 1: I need someone else in my life to be happy.

Inaccurate Thought 2: I only feel complete when I'm in a relationship.

_____

_____

_____

_____

Inaccurate Thought 3: There's obviously something wrong with me if my partner doesn't love me.

_____

_____

_____

Inaccurate Thought 4: I only feel okay, acceptable, or "good enough" when I'm in a relationship.

_____

_____

_____

Inaccurate Thought 5: I can't survive without the love of another.

_____

_____

_____

Example

Here are Fran's responses to the inaccurate thoughts exercise:

Inaccurate Thought 1: I need someone else in my life to be happy.
I guess I really feel this way. It seems as though my life is only bearable if I'm involved.

Inaccurate Thought 2: I only feel complete when I'm in a relationship.

I always feel like there's something missing when I'm not involved.

_____

Inaccurate Thought 3: There's obviously something wrong with me if my partner doesn't love me.

I always blame myself if things go wrong. I never look at the other person.

_____

Inaccurate Thought 4: I only feel okay, acceptable, or "good enough" when I'm in a relationship.

It's sad to say, but I think I feel like a nobody unless a man loves me.

_____

Inaccurate Thought 5: I can't survive without the love of another.

I act like I can't—I always become super depressed when a relationship ends. It feels like my world is caving in.

_____

Step 3: Choose to Change Unhealthy Reactions to Healthy Ones

Now that you're aware of how you perceive yourself and your partner and your inaccurate thought patterns, you're ready to set goals for moving from unhealthy to healthy reactions and behaviors. Review your responses to the exercises in Step 1 and Step 2. Write a goal statement and an action statement for each step.

Step 1

Goal statement:

Action statement:

Step 2

Goal statement:

Action statement:

Example

Fran is ready to take responsibility for how she feels about herself. Here are her goals for increasing her healthy reactions.

Step 1

Goal statement: *I choose to accept myself more.*

Action statement: *During the day, I will think positive things about myself.*

Step 2

Goal statement: *I choose to become more independent, need the other less.*

Action statement: *Start doing more independent activity each week, such as going to a movie alone.*

Step 4: Release Unhealthy Reactions

To release the unhealthy reactions you've learned, you must a) identify your unhealthy beliefs or the source of your inaccurate thoughts and b) correct these inaccurate thoughts by replacing them with healthy reactions. Complete the following exercise by reading the inaccurate thought and the unhealthy belief that produces this thought, and writing a corrected thought to replace the inaccurate one.

Inaccurate Thought	Unhealthy Belief	Corrected Thought
1. I need another in my life to be happy.	I must seek happiness outside of myself.	(For example: I am responsible for my own happiness.)
2. I only feel complete when I'm in a relationship.	I must seek wholeness and fulfillment outside myself.	(For example: I have all I need inside of me to be a whole person.)
3. There is obviously something wrong with me if my partner doesn't love me.	I can't love myself if my partner doesn't love me.	(For example: I am always worthy of love. If my partner doesn't appreciate me, it's his/her loss.)
4. I only feel okay, acceptable or "good enough" when I'm in a relationship.	I'm lovable only when someone else loves me.	(For example: I am always lovable, in or out of a relationship. I love myself.)
5. I can't survive without the love of another.	I am dependent on my partner.	(For example: I can handle life with or without a partner.)

Example

Fran made a real discovery about herself through this exercise. She realized how much responsibility and power she gave to the men in her life. She gave them the power to determine how she felt about herself.

Inaccurate Thought	Unhealthy Belief	Corrected Thought
1. I need another in my life to be happy.	I must seek happiness outside of myself.	*I can create my own happiness. I don't need Jeff in my life to be happy.*
2. I only feel complete when I'm in a relationship.	I must seek wholeness and fulfillment outside myself.	*I must make myself feel "whole."*
3. There is obviously something wrong with me if my partner doesn't love me.	I can't love myself if my partner doesn't love me.	*If Jeff doesn't love me, that's his problem and his loss. I'm okay.*
4. I only feel okay, acceptable, or "good enough" when I'm in a relationship.	I'm lovable only when someone else loves me.	*I'm always okay, acceptable, and good enough.*
5. I can't survive without the love of another.	I am dependent on my partner.	*I want to be with Jeff but I can handle being without him.*

Step 5: Learn and Practice Healthy Reactions

Now that you've released your other-enhancing thoughts you are ready to incorporate self-enhancing thoughts into your thinking process. There are two parts in this step. Part A consists of self-enhancing thoughts to be written and repeated. Part B is a visualization exercise in which you get in touch with the "real" you.

Part A: These self-enhancing statements are a powerful tool for changing your perception about yourself. They can help you to gain a new perception and appreciation of the person you really are. These statements may not feel "true" for you initially; however, you should continue to write and repeat them until you believe they are true for you.

Below you will find a list of self-enhancing statements. Choose one that you will write 20 times each day for one month, and repeat silently or out loud during the day, 50-100 times. The next month, choose another thought, and so on. Continue to write and repeat these statements until you feel that they are true for you.

1. I am beautiful.

2. I am lovable.

3. I am capable.

4. I am powerful.

5. I deserve love.

6. I am worthy of love.

Example

Fran wants to enhance her feelings about her physical self. Each day she looks into her eyes in the mirror and repeats, "I am beautiful." She also writes this statement 20 times a day. Fran is now starting to believe that she is truly a beautiful human being, both inside and outside.

Part B: Visualization Exercise: The Real Me

Below is a poem that you can record on tape to play during this exercise. Sit comfortably, place your feet flat on the floor, place your arms at your sides or on your lap. Close your eyes, take a few deep breaths, and feel yourself begin to relax. When you feel relaxed, turn on the tape.

The Real Me

When I open my eyes, I can see, the real me, the real me. (Imagine seeing yourself standing before you. See yourself as a radiant, self-confident person.)

I am beautiful, I am lovable, yes I see, the real me. (See the beauty in yourself; see the beauty in your physical self and in your inner self.)

When I open my eyes, I can see, the real me, the real me. (See yourself as a person who is worthy and deserving of love. Imagine being hugged.)

I am capable, I am powerful, yes I see, the real me. (See yourself as being capable and competent; feel yourself taking responsibility for your feelings; feel the power that you possess.)

When I open my eyes, I can see, the real me, the real me. (See yourself as a beautiful, lovable, capable, and powerful individual. See yourself in the act of being capable and powerful. Know that the good feelings that you have about yourself now are feelings about the person you really are. Imagine a "you" that has let go of all dependence, all power-lessness, all feelings of unworthiness. See yourself as the independent, self-reliant, self-confident, and self-loving person you are.)

When I open my eyes, I can see, the real me, the real me. (Hold this picture, the picture of the "real" you, in your mind for a few moments. Now open your eyes. Turn off the tape. Practice this visualization often so that you can begin to see and feel the real you. Whenever you are feeling fearful or anxious, visualize the beautiful, lovable, capable, and powerful you.

Step 6: Evaluate Your Progress and Reward Your Successes

As you practice enhancing the self, you will notice that you will perceive yourself in a more positive way. You will start to feel like the independent, confident, and lovable person you are. Complete the following exercise after you have completed all of the steps in the self-enhancement process. Check the items that apply to you and react to them.

As I learn to react appropriately to my partner and our relationship, I am experiencing the following more frequently:

1. I desire rather than need the other in my life.

2. I take responsibility for my feelings.

3. I choose to feel good about myself.

4. I don't expect others to make me feel good about myself.

5. I accept myself whether or not I am in a relationship.

6. I know that I am lovable.

Reactions:_____

_____

_____

My Reward:_____

_____

Example

Fran has noticed a definite change in her thought patterns. She is starting to accept responsibility for her feelings—she is choosing to feel good about herself. Each day it becomes easier for Fran to repeat positive statements about herself. She is liking and appreciating herself more. She is discovering a person (within her) that she respects more each day. Here are Fran's reactions:

Reactions: *I'm starting to feel a freedom that I've never felt before—I feel less dependent on the man in my life for my good feelings. I can and do feel that I like myself.*

My Reward: *I just bought tickets for an off-Broadway play that is coming to town—I'm excited.*

Further Reading

Hay, Louise L. *You Can Heal Your Life*. Santa Monica, CA: Hay House, 1984.

6

Self-Validation

Fall in love
with yourself and
you will always have love.

You will never again
have to fear
being abandoned.

The key to being able to establish and maintain healthy love relationships lies in learning to love yourself. Loving yourself is self-validation. When you validate yourself, you accept and approve of yourself. As a self-validating individual, you can enter into a relationship free of baggage from the past. Your relationship can be based on the desire for mutual sharing and growth, rather than on need and dependency. When you validate yourself instead of seeking validation from another, you give yourself the power to choose how you will respond to your partner, and to maintain your sense of self in the relationship.

If you are addicted to love or to relationships, you have learned to seek validation from your partner in close relationships. It's only through relating to, being involved with, and being loved by the other that you feel any sense of acceptance and approval of yourself. This chapter emphasizes accepting, approving of, and loving yourself. It is about self-validation rather than other-validation. You'll learn the three steps necessary for self-validation. The exercises that you complete will help you take responsibility for this validation process. When you've learned how to cherish yourself, it will be possible for you to find and maintain a healthy relationship.

Self-Validation

Self-validation involves accepting and approving of yourself. It is learning to do for the self what you have needed and expected the other to do for you. In learning to validate yourself, you will have to unlearn erroneous beliefs you have learned about loving yourself and others. Learning to validate yourself can be a tough job. It requires both determination and discipline. Before beginning this process, keep these thoughts in mind:

- Understand the erroneous belief system under which you are now operating. Other-validation implies that you are unworthy and undeserving of love; it is only the presence of, and your involvement with, the other that makes you worthy of acceptance and approval. Under this belief system, it is someone outside of yourself—the other—who makes you lovable. This premise may not be one that you consciously or readily accept as operating in your life; however, if you are overacting to your partner, you are seeking other-validation. To learn to validate yourself, you must become aware of—and then refute—the belief that you are unworthy or undeserving of love.

- Forget everything you ever learned about self-love being selfish. Healthy self-love is the most desirable state to which an individual can aspire. It is not egotistical or narcissistic (both types of love which are negative states in which the individual does not really love the self). If you are to validate yourself, you must accept the belief that self-love is a positive and healthy human attribute.

- Understand that validating yourself is your responsibility alone. No one else can make you accept and approve of yourself more than on a temporary basis. When he or she withdraws love, you will feel as empty as you did before. To learn to validate yourself, you must give up depending on anyone else to love you, and take responsibility for loving yourself.

- Trust the process of self-validation. Choose to learn to love yourself. Consistently complete the exercises. Be patient. Watch the "real" you unfold. Remember—if you can learn to love yourself, it will be easier to find the loving relationship you desire.

The Self-Validation Process

The self-validation process consists of three steps: 1) accepting yourself, 2) appreciating yourself, and 3) acting loving toward yourself. Completion of all the steps is essential to the process. The steps and the exercises included in this chapter are designed to help you:

- become aware of and refute the erroneous belief that you are unworthy or undeserving of love
- accept self-love as a positive attribute
- accept responsibility for loving yourself

Step 1: *Accept yourself.* Self-acceptance is a precondition for change, the key that unlocks the door to self-love. You can't move forward until you accept yourself, and learn to accept the person you are *now.* You must accept the overweight you as readily as the you who is ten pounds lighter; the you that is struggling to become a singer as readily as the you who has become a star; the you that obsesses about your partner as readily as the healthy person you want to become. This acceptance doesn't mean that you don't want to make improvements—but rather that you accept the reality of who you are at this moment in time.

Step 2: *Appreciate yourself.* Self-discovery is the key to self-appreciation. Becoming aware of the unique or special qualities you possess is an essential part of learning to validate yourself. When you appreciate yourself, you focus on your strengths. Your goal is never perfection, but rather to uncover and praise what is positive.

Step 3: *Act loving toward yourself.* Acting in ways that reflect self-love is the final step in the self-validation process. Your actions show respect and concern for your own well-being. You can act loving toward yourself in two ways: by saying positive things about yourself and by giving to yourself. Begin to act like the healthy person you want to become. Soon you'll discover that treating yourself in a loving manner is no longer an act—it is part of you. Remember also that you teach others how to treat you. If you act as if you love yourself, then others will treat you as someone worthy of their respect and attention.

Step 1: Accept Yourself

Part A: In the spaces below, list those qualities which you consider to be your imperfections or defects. Think of any "imperfection" in your physical person (for example, fat thighs or bad skin) and in your emotional make-up or personality (for example, dishonesty, paranoia, a tendency to drink too much). This exercise may seem a little awkward at first, because you are being asked to list your negative qualities. But this is a necessary part of the recovery process. Before you can fully love yourself, you must accept and approve of yourself exactly as you are now.

1.   6.

2.   7.

3.   8.

4.   9.

5.   10.

Part B: Now that you've listed what you consider to be your negative qualities, you must begin to work on accepting these "imperfections." For each negative attribute listed, write the following statement: "I accept my [negative attribute]. It is a part of me. I accept all of me."

1. _____

   _____

2. _____

3. _____

4. _____

5. _____

6. _____

7. _____

8. _____

9. _____

10. _____

Part C: Each day, repeat a general acceptance statement, "I accept myself just as I am," and choose one imperfection from your list in Part B to repeat. Verbalize your self-acceptance 10 times at least 3 times per day—especially on awakening and going to bed. Repeat this exercise daily for one month. Afterwards, repeat it as often as necessary—when you don't feel good about yourself, or when you notice that you're seeking validation from others.

Example

Fran has decided to break the pattern of waiting for the man in her life to validate her. She most recently experienced a sense of loss when her boyfriend Jeff withdrew his love and his accompanying validation. Fran has chosen to use the energy that she usually puts into getting

Jeff to love her into loving herself instead. Here are Fran's responses to Parts A, B, and C of the self-acceptance exercises.

Part A:

1. *too short*
2. *need to lose 10 pounds*
3. *drab hair*
4. *disorganized*
5. *procrastination*
6. *love addict*
7. *temper*
8. *afraid to take risks*
9. *shy*
10. *fearful*

Part B:

1. *I accept my height. It is a part of me. I accept all of me.*

2. *I accept my weight. It is a part of me. I accept all of me.*

3. *I accept my hair. It is a part of me. I accept all of me.*

4. *I accept my disorganization. It is a part of me. I accept all of me.*

5. *I accept my procrastination. It is a part of me. I accept all of me.*

6. *I accept my love addiction. It is a part of me. I accept all of me.*

7. *I accept my temper. It is a part of me. I accept all of me.*

8. *I accept my fear of taking risks. It is a part of me. I accept all of me.*

9. *I accept my shyness. It is a part of me. I accept all of me.*

10. *I accept my fearfulness. It is a part of me. I accept all of me.*

Part C: Fran repeated her self-acceptance statements as soon as she awoke, driving to and from work, and before she went to sleep at night. She decided to begin accepting the physical and emotional aspects of herself that she considered to be imperfect.

Step 2: Appreciate Yourself

Part A: You can learn to validate yourself by becoming aware of and focusing on the ways in which you are a unique and special person. In the spaces below, list your assets and strengths. Think about your successes in life; your special aptitudes, abilities, and skills; your intellectual strengths; your education and training; your physical and personality strengths. Be generous with praise for yourself.

1.	11.
2.	12.
3.	13.
4.	14.
5.	15.
6.	16.
7.	17.
8.	18.
9.	19.
10.	20.

Part B: Choose three of your assets from the list. Write an "I am/have" statement for each asset. Place these statements on index cards and keep them with you. Repeat these statements often, 50-100 times a day. Do this for one week. The next week, choose three more assets to repeat, and so on. Continue repeating these statements until you feel very pleased with who you are and what you've accomplished.

Example

Because Fran has always depended upon others to validate her, she had difficulty completing the self-appreciation exercises. She had to work very hard to think of things that were special about herself. She finally came up with a list of assets in *Part A:*

1. *well educated*
2. *good student*
3. *intelligent*
4. *good writer*
5. *logical/analytical mind*
6. *good problem solver*
7. *creative*
8. *excellent tennis player*
9. *attractive*
10. *pleasing personality*
11. *pleasing voice*
12. *pretty eyes*
13. *good listener*
14. *good friend*
15. *good golfer*
16. *attractive hands*
17. *warm*
18. *loving*
19. *determined*
20. *motivated*

Part B: Fran chose the following self-appreciation statements to repeat during the day:

1. I am attractive.
2. I am intelligent.

3. I am determined.

Step 3: Act Loving Toward Yourself

Part A: Below you will find a list of self-validating statements. Choose one statement that you will write 20 times each day for one month. The next month, choose another statement, and so on. Write the statement on an index card and keep it with you. Repeat it often during the day, 50-100 times, for one month. The next month, choose another statement to repeat, and so on. Continue writing and repeating self-validating statements until you've assimilated them.

1. I love and accept myself completely.

2. I accept myself without reservation.

3. I approve of myself.

4. I am good enough just as I am.

5. I love myself just as I am.

6. I am a unique and special person.

7. I would not trade me for anyone else.

8. [Your name], I love you as you are now.

9. [Your name], I accept you as you are now.

10. [Your name], I approve of you as you are now.

11. I have already proven myself. I'm okay.

12. I deserve love.

13. I am worthy of love.

14. I don't need anyone else to validate me. I validate myself.

Part B: Below is a list of words that describe the feelings of love-addicted individuals toward their partners. Think of your current relationship or a recent one. Check those words that best describe how your partner "makes" you feel. Add any words that you wish.

___ 1. wanted		___11. worthwhile
___ 2. masculine		___12. lovable
___ 3. feminine		___13. accepted
___ 4. good		___14. special
___ 5. valued		___15. important
___ 6. cherished		___16. secure
___ 7. validated		___17. excited
___ 8. complete		___18. alive
___ 9. desirable		___19. needed
___10. sensual		___20. beautiful

___21._____

___22._____

___23._____

___24._____

___25._____

How can you give yourself these feelings without them coming from your partner? For each word checked, think of how you can make yourself feel the same way.

1._____

2._____

3._____

4._____

5._____

6._____

7._____

8._____

9._____

10._____

Part C: Individuals who are addicted to love give to others in hopes of receiving attention, affection, and love. Learn to do for yourself what you desire others to do for you. Begin by giving yourself "gifts" of verbal praise and thoughtful actions. You can give to yourself physically (by exercising, eating properly, getting a massage); mentally (by writing and repeating self-validating statements); and emotionally (by choosing to love yourself by letting go). Give generously to yourself! (Add more spaces below if you like.)

Things I Will Give To Myself

Each Day:

1._____

2._____

3._____

4._____

5._____

Each Week:

1._____

2._____

3._____

4._____

5._____

Each Month:

1._____

2._____

3._____

4._____

5._____

In Six Months:

1._____

2._____

3._____

4._____

5._____

This Year:

1._____

2._____

3._____

4._____

5._____

In Three to Five Years:

1._____

2._____

3._____

4._____

5._____

Example

Part A: Initially Fran was uncomfortable repeating the self-validating statements. She would often forget to repeat them and would sometimes feel that it was too much trouble to write them out 20 times. But Fran was determined to learn to validate herself, so she worked through the discomfort. The more she practiced, the more comfortable she became. Fran chose the following statement:

She wrote and repeated daily: I love and accept myself completely.

Part B: Here are Fran's responses to how Jeff "made" her feel. Fran checked the following words from the list:

feminine	*lovable*	*beautiful*
good	*special*	
desirable	*excited*	

Here are some of the ways in which Fran chose to make *herself* feel the way she'd depended on Jeff to make her feel:

I will make myself feel beautiful by noticing and appreciating my appealing physical traits.

I will make myself feel special by giving to myself.

I will make myself feel lovable by telling myself that I am worthy and deserving of love.

Part C: Fran has discovered two things about herself from this exercise. First, she finds it hard to just relax and "do nothing." She's always busy *doing* something. From as far back as childhood, Fran remembers her mother's irritation when anyone was "just sitting around." Fran has also discovered that when she has fun, she's rarely by herself; she has always depended on someone else to create an atmosphere of fun. Fran's gift to herself will be the gift of enjoyment. She has decided to:

Each Day:

1. eat balanced meals
2. exercise
3. take quiet time
4. take a bubble bath
5. think self-validating thoughts

Each Week:

1. go to spa
2. get a massage
3. go out with friends
4. play tennis
5. get extra rest

Each Month:

1. buy something new

2. go to hairdresser

3. get a manicure

4.

5.

In Six Months:

1. take a mini-vacation (skiing)

2.

3.

4.

5.

This Year:

1. take a trip to Mexico

2.

3.

4.

5.

In Three to Five Years:

1. take a trip to Europe

2.

3.

4.

5.

Increasing Your Self-Esteem

As you begin to validate yourself more, you'll notice an increase in your self-esteem. You'll feel more comfortable expressing positive statements about yourself, giving to yourself, and receiving love.

Complete the following exercise after you've worked through all of the steps in the self-validation process. Check each statement that applies to you.

As I learn to validate myself, I'm experiencing the following more often:

1. I accept my imperfections.

2. I do not strive to be perfect.

3. I feel that I am "good enough."

4. I appreciate my uniqueness.

5. I am aware of my assets.

6. I appreciate my assets.

7. I praise myself.

8. I do good things for myself.

9. I allow myself to have fun.

10. I feel good about myself.

Reactions:_____

_____

_____

_____

My Reward:_____

_____

Example

It becomes easier each day for Fran to focus her attention on herself. She has become much more comfortable repeating the self-validation statements. They have now become a habit. Fran slips into negative thinking at times, but generally she's learning to accept and approve of herself.

Reactions: *I am learning to notice and appreciate my "assets." I have many more assets than I thought. I am finally discovering how special I really am!*

My Reward: *A real treat for myself—the works—a facial, body wrap, massage, pedicure, manicure, and haircut. I deserve every bit of it!*

And what if your partner doesn't see all of the positive qualities that you've discovered in yourself? Work on self-validation to the extent that you can say (and mean it!) that "if my partner doesn't appreciate me, then it's his [or her] loss." You don't need the other's acceptance or approval to feel good about yourself anymore. You've taken full responsibility for loving yourself.

Further Reading

Branden, Nathaniel. *How To Raise Your Self-Esteem.* New York: Bantam Books, 1987.

Hendricks, Gay. *Learning To Love Yourself.* New York: Prentice Hall, 1982.

Whitfield, Charles L. *Healing the Child Within.* Pompano Beach, FL: Health Communications, 1987.

7

Changing Addictive Thought Patterns: Focusing on Yourself

He's on my mind all the time. Sometimes just beneath the surface, but always there. All during the day as I work my thoughts drift to him. I wonder what he's doing. I fantasize about what we'll do when we get together. Sometimes I think about what I am going to say when I talk to him. Driving to and from work is when I think of him most. I usually replay our last date or phone call again and again. I analyze his every word and action. It seems funny now that I'm thinking of it, but sometimes even when I'm talking to my friends I realize that I'm really thinking of him. I guess when I'm involved there's no room in my mind for anything or anybody but him.

When you are excessively involved in a relationship, your mind is consumed with thoughts of your partner. His or her words and actions are always on your mind. You may find that your thoughts dart from fantasies about being together forever to analyzing the meaning of specific statements made by your partner. Your thoughts trigger feelings that range from excitement to anxiety. Like Alice in the example above, you probably find that you can't get your partner out of your mind.

This chapter is about helping you to decrease and normalize your level of mental involvement with your partner. Mental detachment is the first step in accomplishing this. Learning to detach mentally can help you to decrease your physical and emotional involvement as well.

The Process of Mental Detachment

For a love addict, detaching mentally means changing the focus of your thoughts from your partner to yourself. It is a matter of becoming aware of your level of mental involvement with your partner and then making a conscious effort to decrease it.

Obsessing about your partner is by now a learned pattern for you—an ingrained habit. You can, however, *unlearn* this habit with practice.

Mental detachment requires both determination and discipline. You must be willing to complete the exercises and practice the *healthy thinking statements* regardless of how unnatural they may feel at first.

The familiar, no matter how unhealthy, always feels more comfortable at the beginning than the new behaviors you're attempting to learn. Face the discomfort of changing your habits, and in a short time you'll notice that you can more easily exchange a *self-focused* thought for a thought about your partner. All habits are learned. You can learn to focus on yourself—but it takes practice.

The mental detachment process has six steps. Each step in the process is necessary and important to your recovery. With each step, you'll come closer to focusing on yourself.

Step 1: *Gain an awareness of your inaccurate thoughts.* In this step you will discover which unhealthy or inaccurate thoughts reinforce your neediness in the relationship, and prevent you from providing self-validation.

Step 2: *Gain an awareness of your level of mental involvement.* Here you gauge your level of involvement with your partner.

Step 3: *Choose to change unhealthy thoughts to healthy ones.* In this step, you set goals for decreasing your thoughts and fantasies about your partner, and increasing those that are focused on yourself.

Step 4: *Release unhealthy thoughts.* Here you are involved in correcting inaccurate thoughts, thought exchange, and thought challenges.

Step 5: *Reinforce healthy thoughts.* At this stage, you repeat statements that reinforce healthy thoughts, feelings, and behaviors.

Step 6: *Evaluate your progress and reward your success.* Here you explore the ways in which your thought patterns are changing.

Steps 1 and 2 are primarily concerned with identifying unhealthy thought patterns and levels of involvement. You'll use the awareness gained in these two steps to help you make the changes required in Steps 3 thru 6.

Step 1: Gain an Awareness of Your Inaccurate Thought

Below are six inaccurate thoughts that can lead to excessive involvement in relationships. Thoughts 1-3 relate to beliefs about abandonment; thoughts 4-6 relate to the conviction that your partner is a necessity in your life.

Read each thought. Then write your reactions in the space provided. As you read each thought, ask yourself how your feelings and behaviors reflect this thought pattern. React to each thought in turn.

Inaccurate Thought 1: If I am not always available for my partner, he/she will leave me.

_____

_____

Inaccurate Thought 2: If I hold on to my partner, I can keep him/her in my life.

_____

_____

Inaccurate Thought 3: If I let my partner, go, I will lose him/her.

_____

_____

Inaccurate Thought 4: Having my partner in my life makes my life complete.

_____

_____

Inaccurate Thought 5: If my partner were not in my life, my life would be dull and empty.

_____

_____

Inaccurate Thought 6: My partner gives meaning to my life.

_____

_____

Example

Alice remembers being addicted to relationships since she began dating. She always becomes excessively involved with the man she is dating. At 29, she has had a series of painful relationships. This time, as before, Alice is involved with a man who is incapable of sustaining a healthy, committed relationship. Alice and Jim have dated for three years; theirs is an "up-and-down" relationship. It tends to go smoothly for a while and then Jim pulls away. This has been the pattern throughout the relationship. About a year ago, Alice became unhappy with the pattern and sought therapy. Now Alice is trying to learn new relationship behaviors and has decided to work to decrease her level of mental involvement with Jim.

Here are Alice's reactions to the inaccurate thought exercise:

Inaccurate Thought 1: If I am not always available for my partner, he/she will leave me.

I feel that I must keep Jim happy if our relationship is going to work.

Inaccurate Thought 2: If I hold on to my partner, I can keep him/her in my life.

I really don't believe this but I keep trying.

_____

Inaccurate Thought 3: If I let my partner go, I will lose him/her.

I guess I hold on because I'm afraid. I've had so many relationships that didn't work out.

Inaccurate Thought 4: Having my partner in my life makes my life complete.

I think I feel a wholeness when I'm involved that I don't usually feel—its like all the pieces fit.

Inaccurate Thought 5: If my partner were not in my life, my life would be dull and empty.

My life is more exciting when there is a man in it.

Inaccurate Thought 6: My partner gives meaning to my life.

I do feel like I really have a "life" when I'm involved.

Step 2: Gain an Awareness of Your Level of Mental Involvement

Part A: Measure your level of involvement with your partner for one week. Complete the chart below by 1) tallying the number of times your partner comes to mind and 2) noting the peak periods when these thoughts occur. Don't try to prevent these thoughts about your partner—just let them occur naturally. This step is important for establishing a baseline of your mental involvement with your partner. It's difficult to "count" thoughts, but give it your best try. At the end of the week, write your reactions to this record of your observations.

Day	Thoughts	When/Where
1		
2		
3		
4		
5		
6		
7		

Reactions: _____

_____

Part B: Analyze the content of your obsessive thoughts for one week. In week two, note the type of thoughts you usually have about your partner. Complete the chart below by tallying the number of times a specific type of thought comes to mind (for instance, thoughts that are a "replay" of an interaction between you and your partner; thoughts that analyze your partner's words or actions; obsessive worry about your relationship; or excessive planning). Place a tally mark under the type of thought that occurs each day. At the end of the week, write your reactions to the types of thoughts you've been having.

Day	Replay	Analysis	Worry	Planning
1				
2				
3				
4				

5

6

7

Reactions: _____

_____

Example

Alice completed Part A of the exercise in Step 2.

Day	Thoughts	When/Where
1	~~THL~~ ~~THL~~ ~~THL~~ I	*Waking up/getting ready/driving to work.*
2	~~THL~~ ~~THL~~ ~~THL~~	*Some at work/driving home/waiting for call.*
3	~~THL~~ ~~THL~~ ~~THL~~ III	*Mostly at home— Jim didn't call until late.*
4	~~THL~~ ~~THL~~ II	*Same*
5	~~THL~~ ~~THL~~ ~~THL~~ ~~THL~~ I	*Same*
6	~~THL~~ ~~THL~~ ~~THL~~ ~~THL~~ III	*Waiting for Jim to call—getting ready for date.*
7	~~THL~~ ~~THL~~ I	*Getting ready for date.*

Reaction: *I had Jim on my mind a lot—especially on day 3 when he didn't call me until late. I really think of him more than this, but keeping track called my attention to it. I think I was trying to think of him less.*

This is what Alice discovered when she completed Step 2, Part B.

Day	Replay	Analysis	Worry	Planning
1	〤〤 〤〤 l	〤〤 l	llll	l
2	〤〤 l	lll	ll	l
3	llll	〤〤	ll	l
4	〤〤 〤〤 l	〤〤	lll	ll
5	〤〤 ll			〤〤
6	ll		llll	〤〤 lll
7	〤〤 〤〤	ll	l	

Reaction: *I spend a lot of time going over in my head my conversation and dates with Jim. I tend to analyze what he says more when I'm worried that something is or might go wrong.*

Step 3: Choose To Change Unhealthy Thoughts to Healthy Ones

Now that you know generally how many times per day you think about your partner and what types of thoughts you have, you're ready to set some goals for changing your thought patterns.

First, note the average number of thoughts you have per day about you partner: _____.

Second, decide by how much you would like to decrease that number and complete the following goal statement:

- I *choose* to think of [name] only [number] times per day.

Third, note the peak periods when you think about your partner, and decide to think of something at these times that concerns only you. Think of what *you* need, desire, or plan for your own life. Now write a goal statement for peak-period thoughts. Here are some examples:

- When I awaken, I will focus my thoughts on_____
  _____.

- As I am driving to work, I will focus my thoughts on _____.

Example
At this point, Alice is ready to set some goals for changing her thoughts about Jim to thoughts about herself. This is how she completed the exercise:

- Average number of thoughts about *Jim* per day: _19_ .

- I *choose* to think of *Jim* only 8 times per day.

- When I awaken, I will focus my thoughts on *my plans for the day; what I will do at work.*

- While I am dressing for work, I will focus my thoughts on *getting well—recovering from love addiction.*

- While I am driving to work, I will focus my thoughts on *getting back into school and earning my M.B.A.*

Now that you have determined your level of mental involvement with your partner and set some goals for changing your thought patterns, you're ready to begin the real work of mental detachment.

Step 4: Release Unhealthy Thoughts

To release the unhealthy thought patterns you've formed, you must identify your unhealthy beliefs or the source of your inaccurate thoughts, and correct these inaccurate thoughts by replacing them with healthy ones. Complete the following exercise by 1) reading the inaccurate thought and the unhealthy belief that produces it and 2) writing a corrected thought to replace the inaccurate one.

Part A: Correcting inaccurate thoughts.

Inaccurate Thought	Unhealthy belief	Corrected Thought
1. If I am not always available for my partner, he/she will leave me.	I will be abandoned.	(For example, "If I give more than 50 percent, he will probably leave anyway.")
2. If I hold on to my partner, I can keep him/her in my life.	I will be abandoned.	(For example, "People can't be treated like possessions. My partner will stay if he wants to—and ultimately there's nothing I can do about it.")

3. If I let my partner go, I will lose him/her.	I will be abandoned.	(For example, "If you love something, let it go. If it returns, it's yours. If it doesn't, it never was.")
4. I need another in my life to feel complete.	I need a partner to be happy.	(For example, "Only I can make my life complete.")
5. If my partner were not in my life, my life would be dull and boring.	I need a partner to be happy.	(For example, "I alone am responsible for creating a full and exciting life for myself.")
6. My partner makes my life meaningful.	I need a partner to be happy.	(For example, "Only I can give meaning to my life."

Example

Alice examined her thoughts about Jim, and was pleasantly surprised with the results of this exercise. She found it to be very helpful in getting her to think differently about Jim's purpose in her life.

Inaccurate Thought	Unhealthy belief	Corrected Thought
1. If I am not always available for my partner, he/she will leave me.	I will be abandoned.	*I do not always have to be available for Jim. If he wants the relationship to work, he will also make himself available.*
2. If I hold on to my partner, I can keep him/her in my life.	I will be abandoned.	*No matter how much I give, I cannot hold Jim in my life if he wants to leave.*
3. If I let my partner go, I will lose him/her.	I will be abandoned.	*If I don't hold on, Jim will have the freedom to make decisions about our relationship without feeling guilty or resentful.* *If I must hold on to Jim, maybe he's not the right person for me. (I never thought of that before.)*
4. I need another in my life to feel complete.	I need a partner to be happy.	*I do not need Jim in my life to have a full, complete life.*

5. If my partner   I need a   *I, not Jim, am*
    were not in my   partner to   *responsible for*
    life, my life   be happy.   *making my life*
    would be dull   *full and exciting.*
    and boring.

6. My partner   I need a   *I can and must*
    makes my life   partner to   *give my own life*
    meaningful.   be happy.   *meaning. No one*
                                        else, not even Jim,
                                        can do that for me.

Part B: Thought challenges. In this part of the exercise, challenge your need to continually think about your partner. Turn back to Part B of Step 2. Record the number of times that you experienced each type of thought during week 2. Challenge your need to obsessively engage in each specific type of thought, especially the ones that occur most often for you.

1. *Replay Thoughts.* Ask yourself:

    a) Why is it necessary for me to mentally replay a conversation or situation when I have experienced or thought of it more than once already?

    b) How will replaying thoughts help me to create a healthy relationship with my partner?

Reactions:_____

_____
_____
_____

2. *Over-Analyzing.* Ask yourself:

a) Why is it necessary for me to know what the other's every word or action means? What am I afraid of?

b) How will figuring out every word or action help me to create a healthy relationship?

Reactions: _____

_____

_____

_____

3. *Obsessive Worry.* Ask yourself:

a) Why is it necessary for me to concentrate on some negative event in the future? What unhealthy belief is the source of my obsessive worry?

b) How will worrying about some future event or situation help me to create a healthy relationship?

Reactions: _____

_____

_____

_____

4. *Excessive Planning.* Ask yourself:

a) Why is it necessary for me to know what will happen in every situation? Can I be sure that everything will work out as I plan it?

b) How will my planning every future event or situation help me to create a healthy relationship?

Reactions: _____

_____

_____

_____

Example

Here are Alice's reactions to the Thought Challenges.

1. Replay Thoughts. *Replaying thoughts of calls/dates with Jim only makes me keep him on my mind when I could be thinking of other things. I really don't see how it helps our relationship.*

2. Over-Analyzing. *I analyze when I worry. I guess I'm afraid that Jim will leave me, so I watch for every cue of his impending departure—but this has been going on for three years and it's crazy. Enough is enough!*

3. Obsessive Worry. *I guess I worry about what I expect. After three years, I guess I still expect Jim to pull up and go one day. It really doesn't help the situation, it only depresses me.*

4. Excessive Planning. *I plan because I want things to work out—but when I think of it—I guess I can't plan Jim's life. Maybe I should just loosen up a bit and let things happen as they will. I will probably feel better—and maybe things will work better for us, or at least better for me.*

Part C: Thought exchanges. In this exercise, you will exchange self-focused thoughts for other-focused thoughts. Write a list of thoughts that focus on you—your interests, needs, and desires—that you can exchange for thoughts about your partner. Substitute these self-focused thoughts at peak periods for other-focused thoughts, or use them throughout the day as a way to change the focus of your thoughts from your partner to yourself.

Self-Focused Thoughts

1.

2.

3.

4.

5.

Example

These are the statements that Alice will use to help her change the focus of her thoughts from Jim to herself.

Self-Focused Thoughts

1. *I am going to use my time wisely today.*

2. *I am using my energy to better my life.*

3. *I am recovering from love addiction.*

4. *I am going to get my M.B.A.*

5. *I need to think of myself more.*

Step 5: Reinforce Healthy Thoughts

After you release unhealthy thoughts, your next task is to teach yourself new ways of thinking about your involvement in the relationship. There are two parts in this step. Part A is a guided imagery exercise in which you can experience letting go; Part B consists of healthy thoughts that you can substitute for unhealthy ones.

Part A: Guided imagery exercise—*A River Trip.* Sit comfortably, place your feet flat on the floor, place your arms at your sides or on your lap. Close your eyes, take a few deep breaths, and feel yourself begin to relax.

Imagine yourself walking down a grassy path. Notice the tall grass on either side of you and feel the freshness of the grass against your legs as you walk through it. Look at the pretty flowers that grow along the path—see the yellows, reds, and purples. Keep walking along this path until you reach the river's edge.

You have reached a beautiful, gently flowing river. A small but sturdy boat is tied to the bank. Untie the boat, get into it, and begin your journey downstream. Don't be concerned about your destination at this point—just relax and let the river's current carry you. Put your hand into the water and feel its coolness. Watch as a school of fish comes near the boat and swims away. Experience the calmness and serenity of the river as you float along.

Look at the river banks, the tall grass and shady trees. As you pass underneath a large tree, feel the coolness of the shade. Enjoy the shade, but do not try to linger underneath the trees. If you try to linger, the boat will stop. Just experience the shade and continue to float down the river. As you round the bend, smell the fragrance of the flowers growing beside the river. The flowers are many different colors. How many different colors do you see? Enjoy the beauty of the flowers, but do not try to pick them. Just experience the flowers and continue to float downstream.

As you float down the river, you notice a large brown object coming toward you. Do not be afraid, it's only a small log. Don't try to move the log, just relax—the boat will turn slightly and pass it safely. You are caught again by the current. Know that you can float down the river without difficulty if you will just relax and let the flow of the river carry you.

Experience going with the flow of the river...it is ever so gentle. Be aware of how you feel as you are floating downstream. There's no need to worry or to hold on to anything. Just experience the flow of the river—experience the shade of the trees, but do not try to linger or hold on; experience the beauty of the flowers, but do not attempt to possess them. Don't try to move logs—just let the current carry you past them. Just let go and go with the flow of the river.

Pause for a few minutes... Experience letting go. Remember that you do not have to hold on—this is a place where you can come to let go, and you may come here as often as you like.

Come back to your room now. Tell yourself that you can experience letting go whenever you desire.

Practice this exercise often so that you can begin to experience letting go. As you learn to let go mentally, you will find it easier to detach emotionally and physically, as well.

Part B: Healthy thoughts. Replacing unhealthy thoughts with healthy ones takes practice and self-discipline. Initially, you'll have to repeat statements that may not sound or feel right. Say them anyway. Soon you'll discover that you've developed *the habit* of thinking healthy thoughts. Below is a list of healthy thoughts. 1) Choose one thought that you will write 20 times each day for one month. Choose another every month and continue the exercise. 2) Write the thought on an index card and keep it with you. Repeat it often during the day for one month. Every month choose another thought to repeat daily. Continue writing and speaking healthy thoughts until it becomes a habit for you.

Healthy Thoughts

1. My recovery is the most important thing in my life.

2. I cannot worry and be well at the same time. I choose to be well.

3. I am directing my energies toward my own life.

4. I am creating a rich, full life for myself.

5. I am creating a life for myself that I would not want to give up.

6. I am creating my own happiness.

7. I have a whole and complete life.

8. I choose to release my fears.

9. I can deal with my fears.

10. I choose to let go.

11. I am free, you are free.

12. I can love without losing myself.

Example

Alice is becoming more and more comfortable with the process of detaching mentally. She has found that writing and speaking healthy thoughts has made her feel more comfortable with Jim. She doesn't feel as uptight anymore and she somehow feels there's a little less tension between them.

For the first month, she chose to write and say the following thought:

I can love without losing myself.

Step 6: Evaluate Your Progress and Reward Your Success

As you begin to decrease your mental involvement with you partner, you'll notice a change in your feelings and actions. You'll experience a new sense of freedom, and sense of your power to control your level of involvement in the relationship. Complete the following exercise after you've finished all the steps in the detachment process.

Check the items that apply to you and react to them.

As I learn to lessen my involvement in the relationship, I am experiencing the following:

1. I don't worry about my partner as often.

2. I can limit my thoughts about him/her.

3. I think of my needs and desires more often.

4. I am making *me* the focus of my life.

5. I am spending less time waiting for calls and dates.

6. I am using my energy to create the kind of life I desire.

7. I am creating a rich, full life for myself.

8. I am learning to let go.

Reaction:_____

_____

_____

_____

My reward:_____

_____

Example

Alice has been trying to lessen her mental involvement with Jim for two months. She realizes that she must continue to work hard to detach, but is pleased with her progress. She has decided to check her progress on a monthly basis. Alice knows that the more she can detach mentally, the easier it will be for her to add balance to her life in the months to come. She will finally create the healthy relationship she has always desired. Here are Alice's reactions:

Reactions: *I am definitely thinking of Jim less—when I do think of him more than I think is necessary, I know how to bring the focus back to myself. I am working hard on "freeing" me more.*

My Reward: *I am very excited about the progress I'm making. I know it will take a while, but with each step I feel better about myself. I plan to get a massage and facial this weekend—how about that!*

Further Reading

Beattie, Melody. *Codependent No More*. New York, NY: Harper and Row, 1987.

8

Creating a Balanced Life

If you want a pretty flower garden, you must water and cultivate all of the plants. If you do not tend some, they will die of neglect. If you water others too much, they will die as well. Your life is much like a flower garden. You must focus attention on all aspects evenly. Too much attention given to any one aspect of your life means that other aspects will suffer. When this happens, you do not grow and develop in a healthy manner.

If you are involved in an addictive relationship, your life is probably out of balance. Like most individuals caught in similar relationships, you are more than likely directing all of your mental, physical, and emotional energy toward your partner. Because all of your attention is focused on this one aspect of your life, other parts of you remain undeveloped. Consequently you cannot grow into the whole and complete person you desire to be.

To be able to enjoy a sense of wholeness and completeness, you must begin by creating a *balanced* life for yourself.

In this chapter, you will learn step by step how to bring your life into harmony. To do this you must find and establish an emotional, mental, and physical equilibrium between all the major arenas of your life.

Life Arenas

The activities in which you normally engage are generally centered around four primary life arenas: work, leisure, social, and personal. Activities in the *work* arena are oriented toward maintaining and advancing your life. Earning money, doing chores at home, and attending school with specific career goals are all activities related to work. The *leisure* arena includes those activities related to *having fun*. Hobbies, entertainment, and avocations are included here. The *social* arena comprises your interpersonal relationships: your partner, your family, your friends, co-workers, and acquaintances. Finally, the *personal* arena is concerned with the *self*. Activities in this arena relate to self-awareness and self-development. They can range from introspection, to reading a self-help book, to exercising and maintaining a healthy diet.

If you're involved in an addictive relationship, you are probably focusing your attention almost exclusively on the social arena. You are preoccupied with activities related to your partner. More than likely you are only putting in the minimal energy required in the work arena. All of your energy is directed toward your partner, so you have little left over to focus on developing your creative abilities or expanding your horizons. Like many other individuals who are addicted to love or relationships, you may not know how to have fun on your own. You may even have learned to feel guilty about *doing nothing*. Your main enjoyment comes from being with your partner. Because you are expending so much energy on the maintenance of your relationship with your partner, it is unlikely that you are engaging in any activities devoted to personal growth or self-development. If you're focusing all your attention on your partner in this way, you are short-changing yourself, and denying yourself the opportunity to have a whole and complete life.

Individuals in healthy relationships consider the relationship to be a part of their life rather than *their total life*. They are able to maintain a relationship while living effectively in the other three arenas. This balanced focus enables them to reach their fullest potential in all four life arenas. And guess what? Individuals who live balanced lives are usually very pleased with the quality of their relationships. Enhancing their own lives enhances their personal relationships.

The Life-Balancing Process

Life balancing consists of four steps. Each step in the process is important and should be completed. When you have completed the exercises in this section, you will have moved closer to establishing wholeness and completeness in your life.

Step 1:   *Gain an awareness of your level of involvement in each life arena*. In this step, you will assess your level of involvement in each life arena.

Step 2:   *Choose to establish and maintain balance in your life*. Here you set goals for increasing or decreasing your involvement in specific arenas.

Step 3:   *Apply the principle of balance to your life arenas*. At this stage, you take steps to increase or decrease your involvement in specific arenas.

Step 4: *Evaluate your progress and reward your success.* This
        step is self-explanatory.

Step 1: Gain an Awareness of Your Level of Involvement in Each Life Arena

Part A: Below is a box representing the four major life arenas. Think of activities in which you typically engage that relate to each life arena. Write these activities under the appropriate column.

Work		Leisure
	1 | 2	
	3 | 4	
Social		Personal

Work	Leisure	Social	Personal
1. _____	1. _____	1. _____	1. _____
2. _____	2. _____	2. _____	2. _____
3. _____	3. _____	3. _____	3. _____
4. _____	4. _____	4. _____	4. _____
5. _____	5. _____	5. _____	5. _____

Part B: Using the boxes below, tally your involvement in each arena for one week. Place a mark for each activity in the appropriate arena (activities related to work get counted in box 1, leisure activities get counted in box 2, and so on. If, for instance, on your first day of the exercise you engaged in three activities related to the social arena, you would put three marks in box 3 under Day 1.

Day 1   Day 2   Day 3   Day 4

1	2		1	2		1	2		1	2
3	4		3	4		3	4		3	4

Day 5   Day 6   Day 7

1	2		1	2		1	2
3	4		3	4		3	4

Part C: Record the number of marks made in each numbered box for each day.

Work (1):_____
Leisure (2):_____
Social (3):_____
Personal (4):_____

Example

Alice is very pleased with the progress she's making in learning mental detachment. She has now begun to concentrate on bringing her life into balance. Here are her responses to the exercises in Step 1:

Part A:

Work	Leisure	Social	Personal
Job	*Shopping*	*Jim (seeing him, talking to him)*	*My "beauty" treatments—facial, manicure*
Course at work	*Watching TV*	*Seeing and talking to friends*	
Study for course		*Seeing and talking to my parents*	
Housework			

Part B:

Day 1		Day 2		Day 3		Day 4	
// 1	2 /	/// 1	2	// 1	2 (	//// 1	2
3 ////	4	// 3	4 /	/// 3	4	// 3	4 /

Day 5		Day 6		Day 7	
// 1	2 /	/ 1	2 ((	1	2 (
3 ///	4	3 ////	4 /	3 /((	4

Part C:

Work (1): *14*
Leisure (2): *6*
Social (3): *21*
Personal (4): *3*

Step 2: Choose to Establish and Maintain Balance in Your Life

Review your responses in Step 1. In what arenas do you notice an imbalance (either too many or too few activities)?

Too many:_____

Too few:_____

Write a goal statement for adding balance to your life during the upcoming week. (Go slowly—don't try to make major changes all at once. Add or subtract one or two activities without causing yourself major discomfort.)

I will increase my involvement in the _____ arena by:

_____

_____

I will decrease my involvement in the _____ arena by:

_____

_____

Example

Alice is planning to increase her involvement in the personal arena by spending at least one hour a day in an activity related to her self-awareness or self-development. She will decrease her involvement in the social arena by learning to do more things that she enjoys alone.

Step 3: Apply the Principle of Balance to Your Life Arenas

Review your goal statements from Step 2. Then write a list of activities in which you expect to participate for the next week, categorizing each activity by life arena. Place an asterisk next to any item that you're adding to increase your involvement in a particular life arena.

Work	Leisure	Social	Personal
1. _____	1. _____	1. _____	1. _____
2. _____	2. _____	2. _____	2. _____
3. _____	3. _____	3. _____	3. _____
4. _____	4. _____	4. _____	4. _____
5. _____	5. _____	5. _____	5. _____

Say and write the following statements as often as you need to during the upcoming weeks:

• I am directing energy into all my life arenas.

• I am creating a balanced life.

Step 4: Evaluate Your Progress and Reward Your Success

As you begin to add balance to your life, you will experience your life as being fuller and more complete. You will feel more in charge of your life. Complete the following exercise after you have finished all of the steps in the life-balancing process. Check the items that apply to you.

As I learn to create a balanced life, I am experiencing the following more:

- I am setting goals for my life.

- I am making plans based on what *I* want to do.

- I am spending time with family and friends.

- I am beginning to enjoy doing things alone.

- I am having fun.

- I am developing hobbies and interests.

- I am taking time to be with myself.

- I am actively participating in life.

Reactions:_____

_____

_____

My reward:_____

_____

Example

Alice is facing a common problem in trying to decrease her involvement with her partner. She's afraid that if she does too much alone, Jim will feel threatened and possibly leave her. But she thinks she has found a workable solution. She'll begin by increasing her involvement in the personal arena. Rather than sitting and waiting for Jim to call or take her out, Alice will use that time to learn meditation, write in a journal, and read self-help books. When she's comfortable doing this, she'll start to do more fun things alone. Alice feels that this is a comfortable way to make changes without changing the relationship drastically.

Reactions: *I never paid much attention to "me" before. I did my usual "beauty treatment," but that was really the only attention I gave myself (even that was to make me more attractive to Jim). Now I am starting to focus on developing myself.*

My Reward: *I am going to simply "do nothing" this weekend. I'll see Jim, but other than that I'll take a long soak in the tub, have a glass of wine, and read magazines.*

Expanding Your Life Space

If you're involved in an addictive relationship, you may be restricting the emotional and intellectual space in which you're living. Your "life space" very likely includes only those activities that involve your partner. In fact, you may be so involved with your partner that you neglect your own interests, needs, and desires.

After completing the Life-Balancing Process you should have a better idea about how involved you are with your partner. As you make an effort to focus less attention on him or her, you may notice that you have more *time on your hands.* By using this time in healthy, productive ways you can expand your life space.

Expanding your life space involves opening yourself to new experiences and increasing your options. It allows you to create your own excitement in life by engaging in activities related to your needs and desires. Such activities provide stimulation and pleasure in your life. Engaging in these activities will ultimately help you feel fulfilled and complete.

Determining what you're really interested in and including these activities in your life can aid in the self-focusing process. The goal of life expansion activities is not to eliminate all activities with your partner, but to help you focus as much attention on *your* needs and desires as you do on your partner.

Life Expansion Exercises

A. *I Want to Do*

List ten activities you enjoy. Consider even commonplace pleasures, such as taking a bubble bath or reading a book. As you engage in activities you enjoy, you'll begin to focus more attention on what makes *you* happy.

1. _____   6. _____

2. _____   7. _____

3. _____   8. _____

4. _____   9. _____

5. _____   10. _____

B. *I Want to Learn*

List ten things you would like to learn. As you begin to learn new things, you will broaden your experience and create your own excitement in life.

1. _____   6. _____

2. _____   7. _____

3. _____   8. _____

4. _____   9. _____

5. _____   10. _____

C. *I Want to Be*

List five areas of self-development in which you would like to engage. You may, for instance, choose to increase your vocabulary, learn to tango, or improve your public speaking skills—let your imagination run wild. Developing the self will build your confidence, trust, and self-esteem. As you develop in specific areas, you'll generally feel better about yourself.

1. _____

2. _____

3. _____

4. _____

5. _____

D. *Life Expansion Activities*

1. Choose one activity from the *I Want to Do* list that you would like to start doing immediately.

   _____

2. Choose one activity from the *I Want to Learn* list. Choose something that you can both afford and fit easily into your schedule.

   _____

3. Choose one area of self-development from the *I Want to Be* list that you will begin working on immediately.

Example

Here are Alice's responses to the *Life Expansion Exercises.*

Life Expansion Exercises

A. *I Want to Do*

List ten activities you enjoy. Consider even commonplace pleasures, such as taking a bubble bath or reading a book. As you engage in activities you enjoy, you'll begin to focus more attention on what makes *you* happy.

1. *Reading magazines*   6. *Going to the symphony*

2. *Listening to music*   7. *Visiting art galleries*

3. *Reading mysteries*   8. *Eating out*

4. *Going to movies*   9. *Acting*

5. *Going to plays*   10. *Shopping!*

B. *I Want to Learn*

List ten things you would like to learn. As you begin to learn new things, you will broaden your experience and create your own excitement in life.

1. *French*   6. _____

2. *Directing*   7. _____

3. *Interior design* _____   8. _____

4. *More about my job*   9. _____
   (for advancement)

5. _____   10. _____

C. *I Want to Be*

List five areas of self-development in which you would like to engage. You may, for instance, choose to increase your vocabulary, learn to tango, or improve your public speaking skills—let your imagination run wild. Developing the self will build your confidence, trust, and self-esteem. As you develop in specific areas, you'll generally feel better about yourself.

1. *Overcoming love addiction (group)*

2. *Increasing self-esteem (group)*

3. *More poised in front of groups—public speaking*

4. *More confident in my job—course at work*

5. *Develop spiritually—greater spiritual understanding*

D. *Life Expansion Activities*

1. Choose one activity from the *I Want to Do* list that you would like to start doing immediately.
   Going to plays

2. Choose one activity from the *I Want to Learn* list. Choose something that you can both afford and fit easily into your schedule.
   French—by tape

3. Choose one area of self-development from the *I Want to Be* list that you will begin working on immediately.

   I want to continue to work on recovering from love addiction. That's my immediate goal.

Alice enjoyed completing the life expansion exercises. She feels that this is an easy way to increase her involvement in neglected areas of her life. She also feels that by expanding her own life she will decrease her dependency on Jim.

9

Changing Unhealthy Expectations to Healthy Ones

What do I expect from a relationship? I guess that I expect not to have to worry about being alone again. I expect that person to be there for me. I'll be secure. I'll have someone who I can depend on. Maybe I just need to know that the woman I'm involved with wants me above all others. I need to know that she's mine—that she won't leave me.

Frank

I guess I've always depended on the man in my life to make my life more exciting for me. When I'm in a relationship, I seem to have more energy. Basically, I'm a pretty shy person, so his friends usually become my friends, and I do a lot of the things that he likes to do. My life is really pretty boring when I am not in a relationship. For me, a relationship means having a fun-filled, exciting life.

Tina

When I'm alone, I always feel as if there is something missing in my life—something missing in me. I look at all of the couples and wonder why I've never been married. I wonder why I'm not in a close relationship with someone. When I'm involved in a relationship, I feel special. I feel loved. I feel like I'm really somebody. I guess I've always looked to the other person and my involvement in a relationship to make me feel good about myself.

Vicki

The expectations you have of your partner and the relationship will influence the health and outcome of all your relationships. Healthy relationships result from healthy expectations; unhealthy relationships are built upon unhealthy expectations. Frank, Tina, and Vicki have all experienced a series of hurtful relationships. Understandably, all of them now have unhealthy or unrealistic expectations for their future relationships. It's important to assess your expectations. What do you desire from your partner in a relationship? What needs do you expect the other to meet? What do you want the relationship to provide? Are your expectations realistic or unrealistic? Are they healthy or unhealthy?

If you are addicted to love or relationships, you will probably find it difficult to know the difference between healthy and unhealthy expectations. You may never have seen a model for a healthy relationship. More importantly, the faulty belief system that you've developed distorts your view of what is appropriate to expect or not expect in a relationship. You may expect too little, believing that you are undeserving of love. You may expect too much, believing that your partner has the power to make you feel secure, happy, and worthwhile. You may even attempt to make your partner behave in a way that fits your mistaken notions of what a relationship should be like. You may relate more to the romanticism than the reality of the relationship.

This chapter focuses on your expectations in a relationship. You'll learn the difference between healthy and unhealthy expectations. You'll also learn how to change the unhealthy and unrealistic expectations you may now have. Remember, all relationships involve expectations. It's only by having healthy expectations, however, that you can establish and maintain a healthy relationship.

Healthy Expectations

A healthy relationship is *reality-based*. You do not have any romantic illusions about what a relationship should be. You're realistic about what your partner can provide. Neither you nor your partner expects the other to be a miracle-worker. You do not expect the other to satisfy needs that only you yourself can fulfill. Both of you expect and know that a relationship takes time to develop— you don't expect instant love. You are patient. You are fully aware of what you're feeling from moment to moment in the relationship. You expect to share with the other and to have the relationship enhance your life, rather than to *be* your life.

You become capable of having healthy expectations of another when you have healthy expectations for yourself. When you accept, approve of, appreciate, and act lovingly toward yourself, you come to expect to give and receive the same from others. When you've created a satisfying and full life for yourself, you expect to share— not gain—happiness from your partner.

What can you realistically expect in a healthy relationship?

You can expect to

- Be accepted for who you are

- Grow and change

- Come to know yourself better

- Be respected, valued, and appreciated

- Maintain your individuality and sense of selfhood

- Share *some* common values

- Share *some* interests and experiences

- Have your life enhanced by the presence of your partner

Unhealthy Expectations

Unhealthy relationships are based on unhealthy or unrealistic expectations. Unhealthy expectations result from unmet needs for security, completeness, and validation. If your early years were characterized by chaos, insecurity, and unpredictability, you probably try to meet your needs for safety or security in your present love relationships. You may feel as Frank did, that you will feel secure if you can just find someone to be yours.

Your childhood may also have left you feeling powerless. You may feel that you need another in your life to make things happen for you—that alone you're unable to create a complete, satisfying life for yourself. You might have the same expectations for a relationship as those expressed by Tina. You may expect your partner to fill your life with fun and excitement. Mistakenly, you may feel that you need the other in your life before you can be happy and experience a sense of completeness.

Finally, your early experiences may have left you feeling unworthy and undeserving of love. You may view yourself as being transformed into someone lovable only through the presence of another. In this case, you're functioning under the mistaken belief that you are not *intrinsically* worthwhile and lovable. You feel that it's only when someone else approves of you, by interacting with you in a relationship, that you are worthwhile. Vicki could only see herself as being "somebody" when she was involved in a relationship. If you are like Vicki, you have the need to be validated by your partner.

When you have unrealistic expectations for a relationship, you tend to focus on what you want to happen rather than on what is actually occurring. You may find yourself waiting, hoping, and wishing for your partner to better meet your needs, when he or she is simply incapable of doing so.

When you have unhealthy expectations for a relationship, you may also focus all your attention on the future or end-product of the relationship rather than on its development. You're impatient with the process of dating and getting to know each other. You want an instant relationship and instant commitment. Because you're afraid of being rejected or abandoned, you prematurely seek a protective bond.

Your unhealthy expectations will in every way affect your responses to your partner. You may play roles that fit your idea of your part in a romantic relationship, rather than acknowledging your feelings. Often you will resort to manipulation in attempts to control your partner and make him or her fit your fantasy. The most common trap resulting from unhealthy expectations is the mistaken belief that you can change the other person.

You're acting on unhealthy or unrealistic expectations when you

- Focus on hopes and dreams for the relationship rather than on what is occurring in the here and now

- Focus on the end result (bonded relationship or marriage) rather than the process of the relationship's development

- Use manipulation (tears, helplessness, silence, or nagging) in an attempt to have your needs met

- Think that you have the power to change another person

Before you can expect to establish and maintain a healthy relationship with another, you must examine your expectations of your partner and your relationship. If your expectations are unhealthy, you must take steps to change them. You must also explore other ways in which you can meet your needs for security, completeness, and validation.

Changing Expectations

To change the outcomes of your relationships, you will have to learn to change your expectations. If you are to establish and maintain healthy relationships, you will have to develop healthy and realistic expectations for them. There are five steps involved in changing unhealthy expectations to healthy ones. You should complete each step of the process.

Step 1: *Understand your expectations regarding your partner and the relationship.* In this step, you will examine your feelings related to the goals of your relationship.

Step 2: *Challenge your unhealthy or unrealistic expectations.* Here you will examine the beliefs that underlie your expectations and will change your unhealthy expectations to healthy ones.

Step 3: *Choose alternative ways to meet your needs for security, completeness, and validation.* Here you will explore alternatives and set goals for satisfying your unmet needs.

Step 4: *Learn and reinforce healthy expectations.* In this step, you will repeat statements that reinforce a new set of healthy expectations.

Step 5: *Evaluate your progress and reward your success.* Here you will examine the ways in which your expectations of your partner and your relationship are changing.

Step 1: Understand Your Expectations of Your Partner and the Relationship

You'll see below a list of six unhealthy expectations. Items 1 and 2 relate to the expectation that the other or the relationship will make you feel secure. Items 3 and 4 relate to the expectations that the other or the relationship will make your life complete. Items 5 and 6 relate to the expectations that the other or the relationship will validate you.

Read each expectation. Then write your reactions in the space provided. As you read each expectation, ask yourself: How do my feelings and behavior reflect this expectation?

Unhealthy Expectation 1: My partner will always be there to meet my needs.

_____

_____

Unhealthy Expectation 2: My partner and I will become one (will be devoted completely and exclusively to each other).

_____

_____

Unhealthy Expectation 3: My partner and I will share and do everything together.

_____

_____

Unhealthy Expectation 4: I will have a more fun-filled, exciting, and satisfying life than I have alone.

_____

_____

Unhealthy Expectation 5: Having someone special in my life will make me a more worthwhile person.

_____

_____

Unhealthy Expectation 6: I will feel better about myself (accept and appreciate myself more) when I am in a relationship.

_____

_____

Example

For as long as he can remember, Frank has been looking for the "right" woman. A few years ago, Frank became desperate to find someone with whom he could have a committed relationship. He thought he had found the right person in Linda. He loved her dearly and gave her everything that was within his power to give. He wanted to do everything he could to make her love him enough to stay with him forever. When Linda left, Frank was devastated. He couldn't understand how, after he'd loved her so much, she could possibly leave him. He knew that he'd done everything possible to make Linda love him enough to stay. From a mutual friend, Frank heard that Linda really did love him, but felt suffocated in the relationship. She felt that she could never love him enough or be all that he needed her to be for him. It was after hearing this that Frank decided to seek therapy. He has since talked to Linda and still wants to pursue the relationship. He has no expectations, however, for what will happen. At this point, Frank is working to free himself of all his unhealthy and unrealistic expectations for relationships. Here are Frank's reactions to the unhealthy expectations exercise.

Unhealthy Expectation 1: My partner will always be there to meet my needs.
I guess I have always loved the woman in my life because of what she could do for me, or how she could make me feel—not for who she was.

Unhealthy Expectation 2: My partner and I will become one (will be devoted completely and exclusively to each other).
I tend to become very possessive in my relationships. I am afraid I will lose her. Maybe Linda was right about my suffocating her.

Unhealthy Expectation 3: My partner and I will share and do everything together.

I always planned everything for Linda and me. I thought that would make her happy.

Unhealthy Expectation 4: I will have a more fun-filled, exciting, and satisfying life than I have alone.
I guess my life is pretty boring—worse yet, I've never done anything to change it. I always expected the woman in my life to do that.

Unhealthy Expectation 5: Having someone special in my life will make me a more worthwhile person.
Somehow, I don't feel like I'm a real man when I'm not in a relationship.

Unhealthy Expectation 6: I will feel better about myself (accept and appreciate myself more) when I am in a relationship.
I tried to make myself believe this. Actually, I was always afraid I wasn't good enough to keep Linda in my life.

Step 2: Challenge Your Unhealthy or Unrealistic Expectations

To change your unhealthy or unrealistic expectations, you must

- Identify the unhealthy beliefs that underlie your unhealthy expectations

- Change unhealthy expectations by replacing them with healthy ones

Complete the following exercise by 1) reading the unhealthy expectation and the unhealthy belief that produced it and 2) writing a healthy expectation to replace the unhealthy one.

Unhealthy Expectation	*Unhealthy Belief*	*Healthy Expectation*
1. My partner will always be there to meet my needs.	I need another to make me feel secure.	_____ _____ _____
2. My partner and I will become *one* (will be devoted completely and exclusively to each other).	I need another person to make me feel secure.	_____ _____ _____
3. My partner and I will share and do everything together.	I need to be in a relationship before I can have a full, complete life.	_____ _____ _____
4. I will have a more fun-filled, exciting, and satisfying life than I have alone.	I need to be in a relationship before I can have a full, complete life.	_____ _____ _____
5. Having someone special in my life will make me a more worthwhile person.	I need another person in my life to feel worthwhile.	_____ _____ _____
6. I will feel better about myself (accept and appreciate myself more) when I am in a relationship.	I need another person in my life to feel worthwhile.	_____ _____ _____

Example

Frank has begun to challenge his unhealthy expectations for his relationship. He is looking for healthier ways to relate to his partner. Here are his healthier expectations:

Unhealthy Expectation	Unhealthy Belief	Healthy Expectation
1. My partner will always be there to meet my needs.	I need another to make me feel secure.	*I don't need my partner to take care of me. I'm an adult and can take care of myself.*
2. My partner and I will become *one* (will be devoted completely and exclusively to each other).	I need another person to make me feel secure.	*My partner and I will have independent lives.*
3. My partner and I will share and do everything together.	I need to be in a relationship before I can have a full, complete life.	*My partner and I will have separate interests as well as shared ones.*
4. I will have a more fun-filled, exciting, and satisfying life than I have alone.	I need to be in a relationship before I can have a full, complete life.	*I can create a satisfying life for myself.*
5. Having someone special in my life will make me a more worthwhile person.	I need another person in my life to feel worthwhile.	*I am always a worthwhile person— in or out of a relationship.*

6. I will feel better about myself (accept and appreciate myself more) when I am in a relationship.

I need another person in my life to feel worthwhile.

I will love and accept myself with or without another person in my life.

Step 3: Choose Alternative Ways to Meet Your Needs for Security, Completeness, and Validation

If you are to decrease your expectations of the other, you must find ways in which you can satisfy your own needs. For each need listed below, write a goal. Then write and repeat out loud the statements based on healthy beliefs. You may wish to write the statements on index cards and carry them with you. Repeat the statements often (up to 20 times a day) for one month. Continue making these healthy statements until you feel you believe them.

Security needs. You can meet your needs for security by learning to take risks, trusting yourself, becoming more independent, and trying out new behaviors. Think of one way in which you would like to start meeting your needs for security. Write a goal.

I will meet my needs for security by

_____

_____

Write and repeat: I am responsible for my own security. I am taking care of myself.

Completeness needs. You can meet your needs for completeness by engaging in activities to expand your life (see Chapter 8). Take up new interests, learn new things, become more involved in making your own life exciting and satisfying. Write a goal.

I will meet my needs for completeness by

_____

_____

Write and repeat: I am responsible for my own happiness. I am creating a full and satisfying life for myself.

Validation needs. You can meet your needs for validation by accepting, appreciating, and giving to yourself (see Chapter 6). Write a goal for self-validation.

I will meet my needs for validation by

_____

_____

Write and repeat: I am responsible for my own feelings of worth. I am loving and approving of myself.

Example

Here are Frank's responses to this exercise:

I will meet my needs for security by
learning to trust my feelings.

I will meet my needs for completeness by
discovering what I like to do (alone) and doing it.

I will meet my needs for validation by
learning to love and accept myself.

Step 4: Learn and Reinforce Healthy Expectations

Below is a list of healthy expectations based on accurate beliefs. Choose one expectation. Write it 20 times each day for one month. The next month, choose another expectation, and so on. Write the expectation on an index card and keep it with you. Repeat it often during the day for one month. The next month choose another one, and so on. Continue writing and stating healthy expectations until you feel that you can view a relationship in a more realistic way.

- I expect to depend on myself to meet my needs.

- I expect that both my partner and I will be independent, autonomous individuals.

- I expect to be responsible for my own happiness.

- I expect to be able to create fun and excitement in my own life.

- I expect to feel as good about myself *out* of a relationship as in one.

- I expect to provide my own validation.

- I expect to give up any attempts to control the outcome of my relationship.

- I expect to change only myself.

Example

Frank is concentrating on learning how to meet his own needs, especially those related to security. He chose to write and repeat the following healthy expectation:

- I expect to provide my own validation.

Step 5: Evaluate Your Progress and Reward Your Success

As you begin to change the expectations you have for your partner and the relationship, you'll notice a change in your feelings and behavior. You will probably also notice a change in your partner. The less you expect from the other, the more free he or she feels to give. As you learn to meet more of your own needs, you'll find that you can *desire* rather than *need* your partner in your life. Complete the following exercise to evaluate your progress. Check the items that apply to you.

As I learn to change my unhealthy expectations to healthy ones, I am experiencing the following more often:

- I am meeting my need for security.

- I am becoming independent.

- I am developing self-trust.

- I feel that I can handle most things in my life.

- I am providing fun and excitement in my life.

- I am giving space to myself and my partner.

- I am developing my own interests, friendships, and so on.

- I am less jealous and possessive in relation to my partner.

- I approve of myself.

- I am providing my own feelings of self-worth.

Reactions:_____

_____
_____
_____

My Reward:_____

_____

Example

Frank has been working very hard on learning to validate himself and to build his feelings of self-trust. He realizes that he has felt powerless and incapable for most of his life. He has always let the woman in his life become the "strong one." He has felt that as long as he provided love, the woman would stay and take care of him. Frank is slowly learning to take care of himself. He has not had an easy time of it, but he feels that he's learning to love and trust himself a little more each day.

Reactions: *I have finally reached the point where I am more concerned with my own recovery than going back with Linda. I realize I won't be able to sustain a good relationship with anyone—including Linda—until I develop a good relationship with myself.*

My Reward: *This is a first for me. I am going to the mountains for the weekend. I'm just going to "commune with nature."*

Before you can develop a good relationship with another, you must first develop a good relationship with yourself. When you're able to accept, appreciate, and act lovingly toward yourself, and when you're able to create a complete life for yourself, then you'll be able to share your life with another and have the healthy relationship you are looking for.

Further Reading

Schaeffer, Brenda. *Is It Love or Is It Addiction? Falling Into Healthy Love.* New York: Harper and Row, 1987.

10

Creating a Complete Life

Everything seemed to change in my relationship and my life when I gave up the notion that Mark had to change in order for me to be happy. His changing really had nothing to do with my happiness or with what I wanted my life to be about. I chose to go on with my life—he could be with me or not. The decision was his alone to make. When I decided to create the satisfying and fulfilling life I desire, my happiness came—and without the degree of struggle I had once expected.

Sharon

To create your life is to own your life. When you make the decision to create the life you desire, you assume responsibility for your life. You give up your dependency on another to provide for your safety, excitement, and validation. You learn to look within—rather than without—for the ways to achieve a satisfying and fulfilling life.

When you assume responsibility for your life, you empower yourself. You take back and use the power over your life that you have previously given away to others. You realize that you, and you alone, have the power to make yourself feel secure, happy, and worthwhile.

Most importantly, when you assume responsibility for your own life, you will spend less time and energy trying to control and manipulate your partner. You will no longer need to try to change the other so that he or she can provide for your needs. Assuming responsibility for what happens in your own life allows you to *desire* rather than *need* the other in your life. In creating your life, you take care of your own needs.

Your recovery process must include taking responsibility for your life. You should at some point choose to create a life for yourself that you will be happy with, regardless of whether or not a partner is part of your life. This chapter is about creating such a life—a life in which your happiness doesn't depend on the presence or action of another. The life you create must be one that gives you a sense of satisfaction and fulfillment. It is only by creating a complete life that you can share that life with another in a healthy and mutually satisfying relationship.

Creating a Complete Life

If you have always looked outside of yourself for a sense of security, happiness, or self-worth, you may not know what it means to live completely. Living completely is feeling that you have it all—that nothing is missing or lacking in your life. When you live completely, you live fully, passionately, and in the here-and-now. You are involved in all aspects of your life. Your life has balance. You enjoy your life.

Living completely also means knowing yourself, knowing what excites, challenges, and energizes you. A complete life is one with purpose, direction, and meaning. You live completely when you assess your gifts and talents, when you discover your unique contribution to life. Living completely is a matter of finding and expressing your voice.

To live completely is to live in the here-and-now. When you live in the here-and-now, you are not responding to messages from the past or feeling fearful about the future. Life is a process. Partaking of that process moment by moment is to live completely.

You are living completely when you focus your energies on creating the life you desire. You're actively involved in developing yourself, pursuing your interests, expanding your life space, finding and expressing your voice. When your relationship is a part of your life, rather than *your life*, and your relationship is based upon sharing rather than need, you are living completely.

A complete life is one that is happy, satisfying, and fulfilling *with or without* a partner. Think of your life as a circle that contains everything you need to feel whole, secure, worthy, and happy. Try to create a life in which there is no lack, in which you feel no *need* for another person to make you feel complete.

Your Life

Whole

Complete

Fulfilled

Satisfied

Happy

If your circle is whole and complete, you can easily join with another's circle to make two expanded lives.

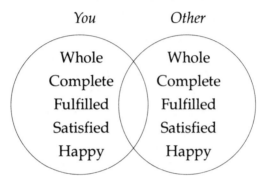

But if your circle is incomplete and you are searching for another circle to make you whole, you can only attract another incomplete and needy person.

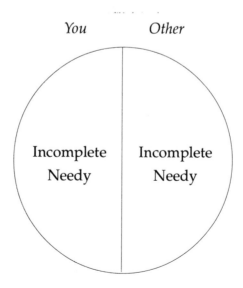

In this configuration, there's no room for growth, change, or expanding each other's lives. You can never become complete in this situation. You will remain half a circle that needs another half to be complete. What happens if the other half decides to leave?

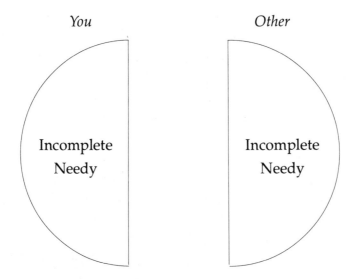

You   *Other*

Incomplete   Incomplete
Needy   Needy

You can't find a whole circle to join if you are only half a circle—you can only join another half-circle. Work to make your life complete and you will attract another who is also complete. Your completeness is the only way to find the healthy relationship you desire. Remember, you can only become whole by increasing the size of your own circle.

Steps Toward Creating a Complete Life

Learning to create a satisfying and fulfilling life is a process. Like any process, certain steps are required. There are six steps involved in this process, all of which should be completed.

Step 1: *Visualize a complete life for yourself.* In this step, ask yourself the following questions: What do I want to do in my life? What is my heart's desire? What life can I create for myself that will make me happy regardless of whether or not I have another special person in my life?

Step 2: *Identify the ways in which your creative energy is misdirected.* Ask: In what ways does my love addiction prevent me from creating a complete life? What payoff am I getting from my addictive behavior?

Step 3: *Choose to redirect your creative energies.* In this step, ask: Is the payoff of addictive behavior worth the anger, frustration, and depression that I experience? Is there a better way to obtain the sense of security, happiness, and worth I'm looking for?

Step 4: *Redirect your energies toward creating a complete life for yourself.* Ask: How can I best use my physical, mental, and emotional energy to create the complete life I desire?

Step 5: *Focus on changing yourself rather than changing your partner.* In this step, ask: Can I really change another person? How can I redirect my energies so that I'm making desirable changes in myself?

Step 6: *Evaluate your progress and reward your success.* Ask: To what degree am I creating the complete life I desire?

Step 1: Visualize a Complete Life for Yourself

Part A: Sit comfortably, close your eyes, take a few deep breaths, relax. Take a few minutes to imagine what a complete life for yourself would be like. The complete life that you imagine should be satisfying and fulfilling with or without the presence of someone special in your life. This is the life that you will share with another *if* and *when* the time comes.

Ask yourself the following questions as you visualize your complete life. You may wish to record the questions on tape, leaving pauses for your answers as you imagine them.

1. What is my "heart's desire"? What do I want to accomplish more than anything else in my life? For what do I want most to be remembered?

2. What is my life's work? What financial resources do I desire?

3. What living environment do I desire? Do I want to live in the city, mountains, by the sea, on a farm, in Paris—where?

4. In what activities, hobbies, interests am I involved?

5. What am I like? How do I feel about myself?

6. In what ways have I expanded my life or enlarged my circle?

7. What steps have I taken to create my complete life?

Visualizing the complete life you desire can help you discover your priorities. Visualization can also be the initial step in creating the life you desire. Visualizing a full, satisfying life that you *alone* create will help you to look within for your sense of security, happiness, and self-worth.

Example

Sharon has taught second grade for eight years. When she did the complete life visualization she saw herself as an author and illustrator of children's books. Sharon sees herself living near the ocean and writing for children. She also sees herself sailing and being involved in the beach life. Sharon does not visualize herself being wealthy, but rather comfortable. She sees her joy coming from living a life that offers her the opportunity to do the work she loves. Sharon's complete life will provide her the freedom to use her creative energies.

Part B: Write the answers to the questions you asked yourself in Part A.

1. What is my "heart's desire"? What do I want to accomplish more than anything else in my life? For what do I want most to be remembered?

   _____

   _____

   _____

2. What is my life's work? What financial resources do I desire?

   _____

   _____

   _____

3. What living environment do I desire? Do I want to live in the city, mountains, by the sea, on a farm, in Paris—where?

⟩

_____

_____

_____

4. In what activities, hobbies, interests am I involved?

_____

_____

_____

5. What am I like? How do I feel about myself?

_____

_____

_____

6. In what ways have I expanded my life or enlarged my circle?

_____

_____

_____

7. What steps have I taken to create my complete life?

_____

_____

_____

Step 2: Identify the Ways in Which Your Creative Energy Is Misdirected

Part A: When you interact with your partner in an addictive manner, you direct your energy into unhealthy, unproductive thoughts and behaviors. They shackle you to the past, often creating chaos in your life. When you're engaging in these patterns of thought and behavior, you're stuck in addiction. You can't use your energies to create a satisfying and fulfilling life for yourself.

Listed below are some typical ways in which mental, physical, and emotional energy is misdirected. Review your responses to the *Inventory of Addictive Thoughts and Behaviors*. Check all the ways in which you misdirect your energies:

____ Waiting/hoping ____ Testing ____ Fantasizing

____ Yearning ____ Game playing ____ Analyzing

____ Obsessing ____ Giving too much ____ Worrying/fearing

____ Blaming (self/other) ____ Role-playing ____ Manipulating/controlling

____ Being overly involved ____ Being possessive

Example

Sharon feels that she has misdirected her energies for the most part into waiting/hoping and yearning. Each relationship she has entered has been with an emotionally unavailable man. She has spent most of her dating life yearning for love and hoping for things to improve in her relationships.

Step 3: Choose to Redirect Your Creative Energies

You don't have to continue to misdirect your energy into unhealthy behavior. You don't have to engage in behaviors that make you feel badly about your partner or yourself. Your unhealthy thoughts and behaviors are related to the past. Choose to live in the here-and-now. From your list of patterns of thought and behavior in Step 2, select one pattern that you would like to change right now. Complete the following sentence: *I choose to live in*

the here-and-now. I no longer have to [name the behavior].
Repeat this statement to yourself often.

Example

Sharon has chosen to no longer yearn for love and attention. She feels that there is no longer a place in her life for yearning for a man who cannot sustain a healthy relationship.

Step 4: Redirect Your Energies Toward Creating a Complete Life for Yourself

Make the choice to use your energies to enhance your life. Think about, plan, and become actively involved in creating the complete life you visualized.

Part A: Review the responses you made to questions 6 and 7 in Step 1.

Part B: Rewrite your responses as goals.

Example

Sharon has chosen to enhance her life by taking the risk of doing what she truly desires in life. She has grown tired of teaching and wants to help children develop through her writing. Sharon also feels that she has the potential to do far more than she is doing now. In the past, she has found it safer to wait for the right man than to risk creating the life she wanted. Her goals are to

- Join a local writer's group

- Attend a local writers' conference to gain more knowledge about writing for children

- Write and illustrate her first children's book within a year

- Look for a beach-house or apartment near the water—start saving to make a move

Step 5: Focus on Changing Yourself Rather Than Your Partner

Often the most difficult part of this process is learning to change yourself rather than trying to change someone else. You can't begin to create a complete life for yourself until *you* change. When you change yourself, your relationship will also change.

Part A: List the problem behaviors in which you and your partner engage in your relationship:

You	Your Partner

Part B: List the behaviors that you want your partner to change:

_____

_____

_____

_____

Part C: List the behaviors you have tried to get your partner to change without success:

_____

_____

_____

_____

Part D: List your behaviors that you plan to change. Use the energy that you were focusing on your partner to change yourself, so that you can create the life you desire.

_____

_____

_____

Reactions:_____

_____

_____

_____

Example

Sharon has finally decided that trying to change Mark is a losing proposition. He only changes long enough to appease her, then returns to his usual behavior. Here are her responses.

Part A: List the problem behaviors in which you and your partner engage in your relationship:

You	Your Partner
Communicating indirectly	*Sending mixed messages*
Holding in feelings until I "explode"	*Deliberately being unpredictable*
Talking rather than acting	*Inconsistent behavior— gets close and then moves away*

Part B: List the behaviors that you want your partner to change:

Mark and I have had many discussions about the "relationship." I have tried to get him to engage in some sort of consistent behavior.

Part C: List the behaviors you have tried to get your partner to change without success:

All of the above!

Part D: List your behaviors that you plan to change.

I will not discuss the relationship anymore—we never come to any resolutions; nothing ever changes.

I will work on saying what I really feel, then following thru.

Reactions: *I don't think Mark will ever change. He just keeps promising that things will be better in the future. The future never comes. I am going to put my energy to better use.*

Step 6: Evaluate Your Progress and Reward Your Success

As I learn to take responsibility for my life, and to focus on changing myself rather than my partner, I am experiencing the following more often:

- I am engaging in activities and interests that I enjoy.

- I am pursuing my life's work.

- I am discovering what I want my life to be about.

- I am looking within for my security, happiness, and validation.

- I am taking my life off hold (no longer waiting and hoping for my partner to change).

- I am becoming more independent and self-reliant.

- I am living in the here-and-now.

- I am focusing on myself (no longer trying to manipulate or control my partner).

- I am developing and expanding my "circle."

- I am choosing to think, feel, and behave differently.

- I am creating a life that I will enjoy alone or with another.

- I am viewing my life as a great adventure, one with new options each day.

Reactions:_____
_____
_____
_____

My Reward:_____
_____
_____

Example

Sharon is very excited about creating the type of life that she wishes to live. She has decided to go on with her life, leaving it up to Mark to join her if he chooses.

Reactions: *Yes, there are times when I miss Mark. But when I think about it, I wonder what I'm missing. We really didn't have a good relationship. I know that I can't go back to being in a relationship like that one. The only thing to do is to go forward with my own life.*

My reward: *I really deserve a special treat for two reasons. One, I finally let go of an unhealthy relationship (I hope the last unhealthy one for me), and I am creating the life I deserve. I am going to splurge and spend a weekend at the beach. I will start to look for a beach-house while I'm there. I am finally taking charge of my life. It feels great!*

When you decide to create a complete life, you will discover that both you and your relationship will change. First, you will change. You will notice changes in the way you think, feel about yourself, and behave. When you begin to create a complete life for yourself, you will feel a sense of

- *Empowerment.* You'll know that you can take charge of your life. You will feel that you can make things happen in your life—you can get what you want. Most importantly, you will know that you have the power within you to change old, destructive ways of thinking, feeling, and acting. You will discover your power to change.

- *Freedom.* With empowerment comes freedom. You'll discover that you really do have options. You can *choose* how to think, feel, or act. You can *choose* to leave or stay in the relationship. You can *choose* how to be in the relationship. You can *choose* to desire rather than need your partner.

- *Confidence and competence.* You'll feel more capable in general. You'll trust yourself more. You'll know that you can handle whatever comes in your life. You will not ever feel compelled to stay in a bad relationship again because you fear being alone. You will know that you are whole and complete within yourself.

- *Honesty and authenticity.* Now you are free of the need to play roles. You can express who you really are. You'll discover and express your true identity more each day. Because you know that you can handle whatever comes in your life, you can live more honestly.

- *Self-approval and self-love.* You'll feel more lovable and worthy than you have ever felt before. Most importantly, you'll find that the love and approval that you sought from your partner was within you all the time. As you begin to enlarge your "circle," you will give yourself the validation that you need.

Your relationship will also change. One of three things will occur:

- *The relationship will improve.* Your partner will notice the new independent, self-confident you and will be more attracted to you.

- *Your partner will leave.* Your partner may be so unhealthy that he or she cannot tolerate your behaving in any way other than the old, unhealthy patterns. He or she may resist your efforts to change, and finally leave the relationship.

- *You will leave.* You may find that you have grown to the extent that you can no longer tolerate the level of sickness in the relationship or in your partner. Because you are healthier, you will seek a healthier person with whom to share a relationship. You will look for another "complete circle" to complement your own.

Further Reading

Small, Jacqueline. *Transformers: Therapists of the Future.* Los Angeles: DeVorrs, 1986.

11

Endings, In Betweens, and Beginnings

If you have read the previous chapters and completed the exercises, you are now either involved in, or ready for, major changes to take place in your relationship. Because *you* have changed, change will necessarily occur in your relationship. You cannot be a self-loving, self-trusting, and self-validating individual while remaining in an unhealthy relationship. As you take responsibility for your own life, you will have less desire and need for an unhealthy partner. As you relinquish the past and live in the here-and-now, you will come to place more value on actions than words. As you enlarge the circle representing your life, you will ready yourself to share life with another whole individual who is capable of returning your love.

The strategies and exercises thus far have all been related to actual involvement in the relationship. This chapter will focus on three other aspects of the process of relationships: endings, the times in between relationships, and beginnings. Each aspect of the process is different, requiring different thought patterns and behaviors. Endings are a time to *let go*. The times in between are for developing a better relationship with yourself. Beginnings are a time to try out new, healthier behaviors. All the new thought and behavioral patterns that you've learned can be used in each of these three phases of relationships.

Endings

The end had been coming for a while. I never had the courage to end it before. Then one day, it happened. I let myself see—I mean really see. I knew that Harriet and I would never have the kind of relationship that I desired. Deep down inside I knew that she simply could not make a commitment. All of her actions and even at times her words said it loud and clear. Somehow, all the time before, I thought I would change her. But that day, I saw, I believed, and I acted. I left, and I never went back.

John

Fortunately or unfortunately (depending on you perspective), your relationship may one day have to end. It's to be hoped that the ending will result from changes that you yourself have initiated in your life. Whatever the circumstances, always consider the ending of one relationship to be the beginning of another, healthier one. If the end has come because of changes you've made, you've no doubt learned some lessons that will help to make you a healthier and better partner in your next relationship.

The key issue in leaving a relationship is *knowing when to leave*. You can make your leaving a healthy and growth-producing act by knowing when and how to leave. Below are some suggestions for leaving a relationship:

- You have already stayed too long if you are suffering physical or mental abuse. Anytime your life, health, or well-being is threatened, leaving is appropriate.

- When you know that no movement, change, or growth can occur in the relationship, it is time to leave. The longer you stay, the smaller your circle becomes.

- Follow your intuition. Listen to your deepest feelings. You will *know* when it's time to leave—there will be no doubt in your mind.

- Work to build your self-esteem before you leave. The better you feel about yourself, the less you will need another unhealthy relationship.

- Have good things happening in other arenas of your life. As you enlarge your circle, the loss of your partner will diminish in its importance.

- Expect to feel some sadness (but not devastation) about leaving the relationship. You are experiencing a loss. Know that you can handle it.

- Know that in time you will attract a healthier partner because *you* are healthier.

- Do not leave simply to go to another relationship. Take time to examine the past relationship and to see in what ways you can change so that you attract a healthier partner next time.

- If your life, health, or well-being is *not* threatened, consider staying in the relationship long enough to learn more about yourself and to practice new, healthier behaviors.

- Join a support group or talk to supportive friends. This will help to reinforce your feeling that you've made the right decision, even when you're feeling lonely and down.

- Practice the strategies you've learned in this workbook. Thought-stopping and thought exchange can make letting go easier.

- Think of the ending as an opportunity to begin a new life. Be open to the options that lie ahead.

- Brush up on your assertiveness skills. Expect that your partner might challenge your decision to leave. He or she may make promises and even try to change. Try to recognize when change is genuine and when old patterns are simply repeating themselves.

- If you don't feel that you can leave all at once, slowly disengage. Leaving permanently or entirely can be kept in mind as a goal.

Analyzing the Ending

All relationships (even the bad ones) teach us lessons about ourselves and how we relate to others. When a relationship ends, take time to see what lessons you've learned. Answer the following questions:

- How was this relationship similar to all of my previous relationships?

- How was this relationship different?

- What patterns am I repeating?

- What tapes am I continuing to listen to?

- In what ways have I grown since my last relationship?

- How must I change in order to have a healthier relationship?

Example

John discovered that Harriet was really like all the other women whom he'd dated. As with all the others, he thought Harriet was different until the relationship started to progress. Harriet liked the good times, the gifts, and the loans that John would make to her when she had financial problems (which was often). He finally realized that he was always giving 90 percent in his relationship—usually to women who were not what he desired.

John has become aware that his faulty beliefs about love and relationships are causing him problems. He always believed that if he just gave or loved enough, he could make the other person love him in return. He believed that if he gave enough, the other could not possibly leave him.

Unfortunately, it took John a while to see that this was a fallacy. Each woman eventually left him. The only thing different about his relationship with Harriet was that he discovered the pattern and acted to end it sooner. John knows that he will have to change his beliefs about love and relationships before he can be part of a healthy and truly loving one.

In Between

I always started to look for a replacement as soon as things began to go wrong in my relationships. They never seemed to change—each one was almost a carbon copy of the previous one. Finally it dawned on me that I needed to take some time to look at what was happening. I decided to just be with myself for a while. I discovered that being alone wasn't as horrible as I'd imagined. It was actually nice getting to know myself for a change.

Cindy

The period between the end of one relationship and the beginning of another is a good time for building a better relationship with yourself. This is not the time to go desperately seeking a replacement for your old partner. In fact, the more anxious you are to find another relationship, the more you need to take time to build a relationship with yourself. During the in-between time, work on discovering who you are. Explore your life purpose. Build your self-esteem. Expand your life, renew or develop new interests, and learn to give to yourself.

There are many paths to building a healthier relationship with yourself. Some of these are suggested below:

- *Meditate.* Be quiet. Calm all of those racing thoughts. Listen to the voice within. Seek direction and guidance.

- *Keep a journal.* Writing is an excellent way to discover and express your feelings.

- *Develop spiritually.* Asking for guidance from a higher power can be very beneficial in helping you to know yourself and the power that lies within you.

- *Develop your intuition.* Learn to listen to your feelings. You have probably learned to ignore your feelings; now is the time to experience them.

- *Join a self-help group or see a therapist (if you feel you want to).* You may have discovered some issues on which you still need to work.

- *Read self-help books (like this one).* Learning new relationship skills can increase your ability to interact in healthy ways.

- *Practice relaxation exercises.* Learn to relax—to take it easy. Use relaxation exercises to help you cope with those times when old anxieties return.

- *Practice visualization.* Visualize your *complete* life often. Imagine your life as satisfying and fulfilling.

- *Practice good health habits.* Focus attention on your diet, exercise, and general well-being.

- *Practice positive self-statements.* Verbalize your love and trust of self.

- *Balance your life.* Engage in activities from each life arena.

- *Expand your life.* Develop new interests. Learn new things. Try something you've always dreamed of doing.

The time in between relationships is a good time to "fall in love" with yourself. Focus all the attention that you've focused on your partner on yourself instead. Give as much to yourself as you've given to your partner. Depend on and trust yourself as much as you depended on and trusted your partner. Love and cherish yourself as much as you loved and cherished your partner. Use the following visualization as a way to help you get in touch with loving yourself.

Falling in Love With Yourself

Sit comfortably. Close your eyes. Take a few deep breaths. Relax. (You may wish to record this visualization.) Think for a moment of your partner; try to recall all the good feelings you had for and about your partner. Allow yourself to experience the love you felt (or still feel) for him or her. Just take a few minutes to *feel* all that love. Now imagine drawing all of that love to yourself. Feel all of that love coming to you. Experience all the good feelings that come to you as you are loved. Enjoy being loved. Feel the same love for yourself that you've felt for your partner.

Imagine speaking to your partner. Thinking of all the loving words you've expressed to and about your partner. Now begin to say those same loving words to yourself. Tell yourself how special you are. Tell yourself the things that you like about you. Tell yourself how much you enjoy being with you. Talk to yourself in the same manner in which you talked to your partner. Experience all the good feelings that come when loving things are said to and about you.

Think of all the loving ways in which you treated your partner. Remember all of the special ways in which you expressed your love. Now imagine doing loving things for yourself. How will you treat yourself lovingly? Imagine many ways. Experience all of the good feelings that come when you are treated in a loving manner.

Think of a special song that reminds you of your partner. Experience the good feelings that song always made you feel for him or her. Now experience those same good feelings as you think of yourself. Imagine dedicating that song to yourself. Experience the love you feel for yourself.

Now slowly open your eyes. Know that you can love yourself at anytime.

Example

Cindy really enjoyed this exercise. She will put one of her favorite songs on the stereo and apply the words to herself. One of her favorite songs is "The Greatest Love" by Whitney Houston. She says that song really helps her to feel good about herself.

Beginnings

After breaking up with Tom, I didn't date for a time. I just worked on building my self-esteem. I went out with friends, got involved in some new activities, and started to enjoy my life again. After a while, I thought I might like to start dating again. I made myself a promise that this time would be different. I promised myself that I would walk away when I met someone who triggered those same old feelings in me. I know now that those feelings are my tie to the past. I've chosen not to live out those old scripts any longer.

Cindy

Ideally, each time you begin a new relationship, you're really starting over—doing things differently. In reality, many of your thought and behavior patterns have been learned over a long period of time and do not go away easily. Even after a lot of hard work on your part, you may find that your old thoughts and behaviors return. You must keep in mind that recovery is a *process* and that you are always becoming a healthier you.

The suggestions given in this chapter are to help you monitor your thought and behavior patterns and show you how the old patterns may creep into new relationships. By knowing what to expect, and understanding why you respond as you do, you can make better choices as you relate to the new partner in your life.

Addictive Triggers

A trigger is a stimulus that initiates a physical or emotional response in an individual. Love-addictive triggers stimulate you to respond in unhealthy ways to another person. They connect you to your past, reinforcing the faulty beliefs about relationships that you've developed over the years.

People usually respond to three types of addictive triggers. Physical triggers are related to physical characteristics and often provoke a sexual or sensual response. Specific physical features such as laughing eyes, small ears, long-fingered hands, or muscular legs may act as triggers. The style, texture, or color of hair may serve as a trigger, or a particular smell or combination of smells. Beards and moles are often triggers, as well as height and build. Vocal and speech patterns, such as hoarse or husky voices or regional or foreign accents, may also be triggers. These physical features remind you of significant others in your life. Often your response to a physical trigger will be that "it turns you on."

Mental triggers relate to *types* of individuals to whom you may be attracted. The type may range from intellectuals to jocks. Types will often make you feel complete because they complement you in some way, or possess a trait that you desire to possess. You can live vicariously through their accomplishments.

Personality traits and mannerisms can serve as emotional triggers, too. These triggers are the most powerful in terms of connecting you with the past, provoking an undefined sense of familiarity. When you meet someone and feel as though you have known him or her for years, you are responding to familiar feelings triggered by certain personality traits or mannerisms. These traits can range from charm or aloofness to the overall feeling or presence of someone's personality.

You respond to triggers in two ways. First, you take notice of the individual. Physical and mental triggers usually operate at this level. Then, you react emotionally to familiar feelings.

Triggers stimulate you to react in habitual ways and repeat old, unhealthy patterns. It's important that you identify your addictive triggers if you are to react in healthy ways in relationships. When you are aware of your triggers, you can make a conscious decision about how you will respond.

Identifying Physical and Mental Triggers

Think of all your relationships in the past five years. (Review your *Relationship Analysis* from Chapter 3 if you want to.) Then complete the following list for each partner in your life during that time period:

Name	Physical Characteristics	Type
————	————————————————	————
————	————————————————	————
————	————————————————	————

Reactions: _____
_____
_____

Example

Here are Cindy's responses to this exercise:

Name	Physical Characteristics	Type
Phil	*Really handsome!*	*Musician*
Bob	*Nice beard*	*Musician*
Joe	*Average*	*Same profession as mine*

Reactions: *I am attracted to "type" more than specific physical features—although beards turn me on. When I think about it, I found Joe to be rather boring. I was really in love with Bob, but he gave me a lot of grief. Phil was really a ladies' man. I see it—I'm hooked on the "artsy" type.*

Identifying Emotional Triggers

There are common threads that run through the relationships of individuals addicted to love. They are usually attracted to people

- Who provide a challenge of some sort (who are aloof, unavailable, and so on)

- Who need help and have troubled lives

- Who provide some form of validation

These common threads all serve to reinforce unhealthy thought patterns. If your partner provides a challenge, you may think:

- *I will be really special if I can make her like me.*

- *I can be the one to change her.*

If the other appears to be needy, you may think

- *I can make him love me if I help him.*

- *I can make him stay with me if I help him.*

If the other makes you feel good about yourself, you may think:

- *I feel good because my partner likes me.*

- *I need my partner in my life to continue feeling this way.*

Review your *Relationship Analysis.* Complete the following for each partner in your life for the past five years:

Name   Emotional Attraction

_____   _____

_____   _____

_____   _____

Reactions: _____
_____
_____

Example

Cindy is noticing a definite pattern in her relationships. Here are her responses to the exercise.

Name	Emotional Attraction
Phil	*Sexy, charming, but could be a little aloof. I remember wanting to make him notice me.*
Bob	*Unavailable—he was dating another musician in his group. But he was so charming. I just wanted him.*
Joe	*Nice, but I don't know if there really was much of an attraction. I wasn't with him long.*

Reactions: *Joe really liked me and wanted a serious relationship—but I wasn't interested. My trigger is the challenge. I tend to want to be with men who I'll have to "work" to get. Somehow it's exciting but always a struggle. I'm tired of struggle—I'll seriously consider the stable, solid "Joe" type from now on.*

You are usually attracted to someone at the same level of psychological health as you are. You attract your "mirror image." Look closely at the person to whom you're attracted. If you begin to feel those same familiar feelings, take some time to do further work on developing your relationship with yourself. The time spent in becoming whole and complete will be well worth the effort in changing the quality of your relationships with others.

Further Reading

Keyes, Ken. *A Conscious Person's Guide to Relationships.* Coos Bay, OR: Living Love Publications, 1979.

Sills, Judith. *A Fine Romance.* Los Angeles: Jeremy P. Tarcher, Inc. 1987.

12

Changing Relationship Responses

You're on—
The curtain is about to open.
What lines will you choose?

Will you deliver the same lines,
To the same audience,
With the same predictable tears?

Or will you change the script?
Play it differently this time?
It's your play.

I hope that the preceding chapters have helped you learn how to identify and change your addictive thoughts and behaviors. This chapter contains exercises to help you see how well you understand your new, healthier responses to relationships.

Romance Theatre provides the format for these exercises. This format consists of a series of one-act plays. Each play's main character is an individual who is play-

ing a role based on false or romantic beliefs about relationships. As a result, he or she is following a script that
includes unhealthy relationship responses.

To complete the exercise, you will write a new script
for each character based on your knowledge of *healthy*
relationship responses. Rewrite the script to reflect
healthy and accurate thoughts and behaviors. Review
Chapters 5-11 if you want to before beginning the exercise.

It's to be hoped that you've already begun the process
of changing the unhealthy thought patterns in your own
life. As you experience situations similar to those in the
exercises, remember that you can *rewrite* the scripts. You
do not have to choose to think or act in old familiar ways.
You do not have to choose thought and behavior patterns
that result in unhealthy, destructive, and hurtful relationships. Just as you rewrite the scripts for the individuals
in *Romance Theatre*, you can change the thought and behavior patterns in your own life. As you interact in your
relationships, rewrite the script—choose a healthier response.

Romance Theatre

Read each vignette and the series of thoughts that follow.
First, give your reactions. Then rewrite each unhealthy
thought to reflect a healthier way of responding to the
situation.The numbers of relevant chapters are identified
in parentheses after each thought.

Vignette I: Laura has been anxious to meet a new man
since she broke up with Tony a month ago. She is preoccupied with where and when she will meet her new
boyfriend. She spends little time alone; rather, she goes
out almost every night. She has gone to singles' bars,

health clubs, and sports events in hopes of attracting a new man.

Laura's Thoughts

1. I am going out as often as possible until I find someone. (11)

   _____

   _____

2. I *have to* find a replacement for Tony. (11)

   _____

   _____

3. I can't stand being alone. My life has been so dull and boring since Tony and I broke up. (11)

   _____

   _____

Reactions:_____

_____

_____

_____

Vignette II: Mark just never seems to find the *right* person. He meets someone, falls head over heels in love with her, and, before he knows it, she's gone. He's beginning to think that there are no "good women" out there. He was introduced to Amber at a party. They spent most of the evening together. Mark has gotten Amber's phone number and is very excited about taking her out on the weekend.

Mark's Thoughts

1. Amber is my dream come true. (5 and 6)

   _____

_____

   2. I wonder if Amber really likes me. I'll show her a
      good time to be sure she does. (5 and 6)

_____

_____

   3. I am really fortunate to find someone as special as
      Amber to go out with me. (5 and 6)

_____

_____

Reactions:_____

_____

_____

Vignette III: Patsy has been dating Troy for a month.
She's been in a state of excitement since they began to
date. She thinks of Troy from the time she wakes up until
she goes to sleep. Patsy has pretty much started to plan
her activities to revolve around going out with Troy.
When she's not seeing or talking to him, she's daydream-
ing about when she will.

Patsy's Thoughts

   1. I hope no one calls me. I don't want the phone to
      be tied up when Troy tries to reach me. (7 and 8)

_____

_____

   2. I think I'll send Troy this cute little card to let him
      know how I feel about him. (5 and 6)

_____

_____

3. Mary won't mind if I don't go to the movies with her as we planned. She should know that going out with a man is more important. (5 and 6; 7 and 8)

_____

_____

Reactions:_____

_____

_____

Vignette IV: Millie has dated Ken for a year now. Her life is pretty much organized around his. Ken works an evening shift. Millie has planned her activities so that she sleeps from the time she gets home from work until Ken gets off at 12:00. Then she gets up to talk to Ken on the phone or meet him. Her life at this point consists of going to work, sleeping, and seeing or talking to Ken after midnight.

Millie's Thoughts

1. There isn't really that much on television these days, so I might as well sleep until Ken gets off from work. (7 and 8)

_____

_____

2. I'm really not interested in anything but my relationship with Ken. (7 and 8)

_____

_____

3. If I'm not available to see Ken when *he's* available, he'll find someone else. (7 and 8)

_____

_____

Reactions:_____

_____
_____

Vignette V: Annie has been unhappy in her live-in relationship with Paul for some time now. She is, however, unable to bring herself to leave him. A major problem is that Paul changes jobs almost monthly. He rarely has his share of the money to cover their household expenses and often has to borrow spending money from Annie. Paul keeps promising that when he finds the *right* job, he'll stick with it so that they can save enough money to get married.

Annie's Thoughts

1. Paul really has a good heart—he has just had some bad breaks. I have to be patient with him. I know he'll get and finally keep a good job. He's capable and, most of all, he loves me. (9 and 10)

   _____
   _____

2. I'll have to stay a little longer. I can't leave now. How would I pay my rent? (9 and 10)

   _____
   _____

3. Once Paul gets on his feet, I plan to go back to school myself. I want to be able to get a better job, but need more skills. (9 and 10)

   _____
   _____

Reactions:_____

_____

_____

Vignette VI: Greg and Jenny broke up four months ago. Greg has been in a state of depression ever since. Jenny had made it known virtually since the beginning of the relationship that she wasn't interested in a commitment. She just wanted to be free. They spent a great deal of their time together quarreling about her going out with other men. Finally she left.

Greg's Thoughts

1. I'll never find another woman who is as exciting to be with as Jenny. She really changed my life. (9 and 10)

   _____

   _____

2. There must be something wrong with me, since I couldn't make Jenny stay in our relationship. (5 and 6)

   _____

   _____

3. This is the worst period of my life. I don't know if, or how, I can ever get over losing Jenny. (11)

   _____

   _____

Reactions:_____

_____

_____

_____

50 Ways to Rewrite Relationship Scripts

Below are 50 ways to help you rewrite your relationship scripts. These suggestions are a summary of ideas expressed in previous chapters. By changing your thoughts and behaviors or your "scripts," you can change your relationships.

- Choose to change
- Set goals for change
- Challenge faulty beliefs
- Challenge unhealthy behaviors
- Focus your attention on yourself
- Accept and approve of yourself
- Appreciate your unique and special qualities
- Acknowledge your personal power
- Trust yourself to handle whatever comes
- Look within for wholeness and fulfillment
- Take responsibility for your own happiness
- Treat yourself lovingly
- Give to yourself
- Learn to play
- Acknowledge and experience your feelings
- Trust your feelings
- Express your feelings
- Let the *real* you emerge

- Maintain balance in all of your life arenas

- Give out of love and caring, not fear

- Give yourself and your partner *space*

- Create excitement in other areas of your life

- Expand your life space

- Take time to be with yourself

- Develop your independence

- Take charge of your life

- Develop and *expand your circle*—create a complete life

- Use your physical, mental, and emotional energy to enhance your life

- Focus on changing yourself

- Give up trying to change your partner

- Feel entitled to a good relationship

- Be aware of your *addiction triggers*

- Walk away from people or situations that trigger unhealthy responses

- Focus on who your partner is (on character) rather than how he or she makes you feel.

- Be aware of relationship *patterns*

- Accept your partner's words and actions at face value

- Judge the quality of the relationship by what is actually taking place

- Live in the *here-and-now*

- Learn to accept gray areas

- Be patient—let the relationship develop naturally

- Focus on the process, not the outcome of the relationship

- Examine your expectations

- Learn to *let go*

- Learn when to stay and when to leave

- Consider a relationship as a means of learning about yourself

- Keep all possibilities open—date others (if your relationship is not exclusive), seek new friends

- Develop a good relationship with yourself

- Monitor your thoughts, feelings, and actions

- Use moments of discomfort (obsessive episodes) to try out new behaviors

- Realize that life is for living, not waiting and hoping

Rewriting Your Script

Prelude to Love
by Martha R. Bireda

Someday, you will discover,
It's really not necessary to bring
Your past with you.
You're all grown-up now—
You can feel what you really feel.

Now, it's all easier to understand,
To separate reality from fantasy
Discard all those false beliefs,
To even learn to see yourself—
As you really are.

You'll choose a new path—
One without all that pain and yearning,
Say no to hoping and waiting,
Decide to live fully instead,
And let others take care of themselves.

Someday, the lessons will be learned,
The healing begun,
You will realize your own power,
And discover that you are finally free—
To simply love.

The aim of this book has been to help you rewrite your relationship scripts. The most important change you must make to do this successfully is a change in thought patterns. The thinking that occurs in addictive relationships is based on faulty belief systems that are established early in life. These belief systems reinforce unhealthy thought patterns, which in turn lead to unhealthy behaviors in relationships.

Addictive thought patterns are primarily based on fear—fear of rejection or abandonment. These thought patterns are very restrictive. They limit you to stereotypic ways of responding in the relationship. They limit you to certain roles, usually that of the martyr or victim within the relationship. Most of all, addictive thought patterns limit your ability to feel and act authentically. They prevent the *real* you from emerging. The person with whom your partner interacts is a you who is ruled by fear and a you who is obsessed with making *things work out* in adult life.

When you choose to change addictive thoughts and behaviors, you are choosing to be the *real* you. You are choosing to acknowledge and experience your true feelings. You are choosing to let go of the past and respond to the here-and-now of your situation.

By changing or rewriting scripts, you are choosing the freedom to create a whole and complete life for yourself. Most importantly, in the context of this book, changing allows you the freedom to love. When you move from an addictive to a healthy orientation, you are increasing your chances of attracting someone healthy to you. You are making it easier for yourself to establish and maintain a healthy, loving, and lasting relationship.

Take a risk. Give up the familiar ways of thinking and acting. Choose to live differently. Deviate from your pattern. Choose to rewrite your script. In choosing to change, you will discover the most important love of all—love of self.

Other New Harbinger Self-Help Titles

The Relaxation & Stress Reduction Workbook, 3rd Edition, $13.95
Leader's Guide to the Relaxation & Stress Reduction Workbook, $14.95
Beyond Grief: A Guide for Recovering from the Death of a Loved One, $10.95
Thoughts & Feelings: The Art of Cognitive Stress Intervention, $12.95
Messages: The Communication Skills Book, $11.95
The Divorce Book, $10.95
Hypnosis for Change: A Manual of Proven Techniques, 2nd Edition, $11.95
The Deadly Diet: Recovering from Anorexia & Bulimia, $11.95
Self-Esteem, $11.95
The Better Way to Drink, $10.95
Chronic Pain Control Workbook, $12.50
Rekindling Desire, $10.95
Life Without Fear: Anxiety and Its Cure, $9.95
Visualization for Change, $11.95
Guideposts to Meaning, $10.95
Controlling Stagefright, $10.95
Videotape: Clinical Hypnosis for Stress & Anxiety Reduction, $24.95
Starting Out Right: Essential Parenting Skills for Your Child's First Seven Years, $12.95
Big Kids: A Parent's Guide to Weight Control for Children, $10.95
Personal Peace: Transcending Your Interpersonal Limits, $10.95
My Parent's Keeper: Adult Children of the Emotionally Disturbed, $11.95
When Anger Hurts, $12.95
Free of the Shadows: Recovering from Sexual Violence, $11.95
Resolving Conflict With Others and Within Yourself, $11.95
The New Three Minute Meditator, $9.95
Liftime Weight Control, $10.95
Getting to Sleep, $10.95
The Anxiety & Phobia Workbook, $12.95
When Once Is Not Enough: Help for Obsessive Compulsives, $11.95

Send a check or purchase order for the titles you want, plus $2.00 for shipping and handling, to:

New Harbinger Publications
Department B
5674 Shattuck Avenue
Oakland, CA 94609

Or write for a free catalog of all our quality self-help publications.